LUCKY HAZARDS

My Life in Physics

MYER BLOOM

ISSS Press
Vancouver, BC

ISSS Press

Library and Archives Canada Cataloguing in Publication
Bloom, Myer, 1928—, author
Lucky hazards : my life in physics / Myer Bloom.

Issued in print and electronic formats.

ISBN 978-0-9938539-1-3 (bound).—ISBN 978-0-9938539-0-6 (ebook)

1. Bloom, Myer, 1928—. 2. Biophysicists—Canada—Biography. I. Title.
QC16.B56A3 2014   530.092   C2014-904749-5
C2014-904750-9

Jacket design by Kevan D'Agostino
Printed and bound in Canada

14 15 16 17 18 5 4 3 2 1

To the memory of my wife, Peggy;
our children, David and Margot;
and our grandson, Alex

CONTENTS

FOREWORD

Ole G. Mouritsen
Professor of Biophysics,
University of Southern Denmark

I met Myer and Peggy Bloom for the first time in the summer of 1979. In that year I worked on the last part of my PhD thesis on magnetic systems. I had already been to a number of international conferences about magnetic resonance, and on several of those occasions I had heard Myer's name being mentioned and the suggestion being made that his lab was a great place to go and work as a post-doc.

I wrote to Myer to make inquiries, and soon I got a nice handwritten letter from Paris where it turned out he had installed himself on a sabbatical leave. Myer invited me to come and work in his lab at UBC and, moreover, he suggested that he and Peggy come to visit me in Denmark in July 1979 to discuss physics and the prospect of going to Vancouver. And so it was—and there began my journey and lucky hazardous venture into the world of biophysics. It was the start of a journey that shaped my life and my career as a scientist, both much influenced by

Myer's approach not only to science but also to friendship and to life as a human being.

There is much to be said about Myer's many contributions to science, which are amply documented in the scientific literature. There is also much to be said about his mentorship of, and collaboration with, a diverse group of scientists from around the world. Many of them experienced the magic of Room 100 in the UBC physics department, where Myer daily discussed the various experiments and their theoretical underpinning and interpretation to the crowd assembled around him, and the discussions often continued over lunch at the Faculty Club. Although many details were discussed, Myer insisted that the focus remain on what he called "the big picture," which meant that fundamental questions in physics and ideas about evolution were considered equally important and interesting.

This wide-ranging conversation about the connections between science and life was internalized by Myer's greater scientific family from near and far, and it was closely interwoven with his own family life. Many of us felt like close members of Myer's family, as we joined him and his wife and children at Chinese restaurants, on the ski slopes or on hikes around Vancouver. For me and for many of his students, Myer has been a role model: his approach shows that a life in science can be a whole life, that family and the relationships between people are the salt of both life and science. It was "lucky hazards" that brought Myer and me together, and allowed me to know and learn from him. I strive in my own approach to science and life to carry on his legacy.

Myer has a great personal and passionate story to tell. These memoirs are a testament to a person who has combined being a scientist and a human being in a unique way. He is a real "mensch," and young and old alike can learn from his story.

CHAPTER 1.

WHAT'VE YOU GOT TO LOSE?

When I was growing up, I had no clear idea of what I wanted to do or "be." In our family, no member of my parents' generation had any university experience, much less a postgraduate education. The kinds of conversations I heard when I attended family gatherings in Montreal were captured by the comedian Danny Kaye in one of his patter songs:

> "Hello!
> How are you?
> How's the folks?
> What's new?
> I'm great!
> That's good!..."

At these gatherings, my older relatives would often ask me, "So, are you going to go to McGill?" I would say, "Probably." The next question they would ask was, "Are you going to be a doctor or a lawyer?" I wasn't so sure about that; perhaps the question came too soon.

When I was in high school I had excellent marks. My parents tried to pin me down about what I might like to do for a living someday, but I was quite cagey about this subject. Maybe this was due to my father's experience of passing exams in a field he would never pursue. When he first arrived in Canada, he was thirteen years old and spoke very little English, but he immediately set out to educate himself. He went to night school to prepare himself for the entrance exams for McGill University. Because he also worked for his father to keep the family business going, he did not have the time or the money to go to university and he trained to be a designer and cutter of ladies' garments. The garment industry seemed to offer relative job security for immigrant Jews, and he chose one of the important and demanding roles. When the Great Depression of the 1930s hit, he was in fact able to keep his job and support his family.

My mother believed strongly that parents should not impose career decisions on their children. When I was about to start high school, she allowed me to choose whether to go to Commercial High School, to prepare for the business world, or to Baron Byng High School, to follow an academic program. I chose Baron Byng, and in 1945, my graduation year, she said, "I was just reading a story in the *Montreal Star* about a group of psychologists who are trying to figure out what influences a person's decisions at your stage of development. Why don't you take their test and see what you should pursue?"

I spent a week punching holes in stiff paper to record my selections—computers were primitive in those days. The researchers did cross-checks on my abilities and aptitudes. On the fifth day the psychologist said: "You are in the upper group in your scores in physics and mathematics. But you should on no account go into physics and mathematics, because you are not in the least bit interested in it." This assessment was based on the fact that when I was asked: "Would you rather visit a science museum or read a novel?" I chose the novel. The psychologist's recommendation didn't influence me, though I didn't disagree with the evaluation of my interests. Indeed, I have sometimes wondered if I should not have been a writer after all.

My attitude was based on ignorance. Much later, I realized that the committee was not using the right criteria. The researchers did not ask themselves if students could have an opinion about something that they knew too little about. In fact, the aptitude test I took was considered cutting edge. Its results showed that I had no interest in physics but I had a lot of natural ability in that subject. So there was no allowance for the fact that if you're successful at something, your interest in that field of study will grow. This might have to do with getting recognition, which often stimulates creative responses.

One might ask whether I had shown a genuine interest in physics when I entered university. My considered answer is "No!" At the time, I thought of myself as just an ordinary guy who was good at school and very interested in sports and recreational activities. Like most good scholars in our community, I just assumed that when I graduated from high school I would apply for admission to McGill University in order to prepare myself for a career of some kind. I did not know which direction this career would take. I was not interested in the conventional professional fields of medicine or law, but I thought

I might consider engineering and had applied to the first year of the bachelor of science program, which was required for engineering.

In the end, events in the outside world—the Great Depression and the end of World War II—had the greatest effect on the direction of my studies. I received a personal letter from F. Cyril James, the vice-chancellor of McGill (equivalent to the university president), inviting me to a meeting in a few days. Dr. James wrote that it was essential that all science and engineering students attend this meeting, as some important information would be provided that affected these programs.

This was late summer, 1945, and student registration was scheduled to take place a few days later. World War II had just ended and the veterans were coming home. Rumours were rampant about what the vice-chancellor was going to say. What he said was that the government had made a commitment to support the returning veterans in any post-secondary programs for which they were qualified. McGill had every intention of providing facilities for qualified students, but the available space at the Montreal campus was not sufficient. However, the university had found a solution by moving the first-year science and engineering programs to Dawson College in St. Jean, which is about thirty kilometres south of the city. This meant that I would be forced to take up residence away from home, and this idea felt like a disaster to me. I had lived with my parents all my life and had counted on living with them while I attended McGill. Their home was only a fifteen-minute walk from the Montreal campus, and the cost of living in a dormitory represented a serious amount of extra expense for the family. I'm certain that my parents would have borrowed the money since they had no savings, but I felt badly about this.

I also knew there was an alternative admission process to doing the first year at McGill, because students who graduated from high school with marks that were not high enough to qualify for entrance to the university could enrol in a Grade 12 Senior Matriculation Program at the high school and hope to perform to a sufficiently high standard to be accepted into the second year of a university program at McGill. The curriculum in Grade 12 was well established and had been in operation for many years, although it had lower prestige than the university program. The Senior Matriculation Program had already started that year, but I didn't worry about having missed the first couple of weeks and I immediately enrolled in it. I was actually very pleased with many aspects of the program, including the fact that students were given the kind of independence usually associated with a university.

In addition, my life was very agreeable, since I could continue my voracious reading of literature and my participation in sports. I also had an active social life, and I was confident that I could handle the academic work with no trouble.

I initially assumed that I would be able to enrol in the engineering program when I was admitted to second year at McGill. However, partway through my year in Senior Matriculation, the university announced that due to the large number of first-year students in engineering, that program would continue at Dawson College. Since I still did not want to go to Dawson College, I read the university calendar for second-year science programs very carefully and discovered that a number of interesting-looking honours programs were offered at the Montreal campus. The one that most appealed to me was the Joint Honours Program in Mathematics and Physics. And that degree is what led me to a career in physics.

As it happened, the twentieth century was an exciting time in science because of the many revolutions that were taking place. The first revolution occurred in physics and began around 1900, when the quantum structure of matter was proposed. This led to a theoretical development, the field of quantum mechanics, which is now well established. The initial flood of ideas came during the 1920s and has continued up to the present day. Although there remain serious disagreements in the interpretation of the theory, it has provided the basis for a complete understanding of atomic and molecular structure. Steady improvements in the speed and precision of computers and computational techniques have contributed greatly, and many new theoretical concepts, such as quantum electrodynamics, many-body systems and strange particles, have emerged. Astronomy and chemistry have also been affected by this new thinking: the field of astrophysics was created and most of the study of chemistry is now based on physics.

The next revolution occurred in biology and began in the 1950s, when James D. Watson and Francis Crick presented a new theory suggesting that human DNA (deoxyribonucleic acid) molecules were arranged in two entwined strands they called a "double helix." This thinking led to the Human Genome Project in the 1990s, which identified, mapped and sequenced the genetic information encoded within the twenty-three chromosome pairs in cells. The sequence of the nucleic acids is called a "genetic code," and it defines proteins accurately and reversibly. By 2003, the Human Genome Project had succeeded in identifying the sequence of all three billion "letters," or base pairs, in the human genome. Impressive as this result is, it is only the beginning of our quantitative understanding of properties of biological materials at the molecular level.

I actually met Watson personally in 1956, a couple of years after he and Crick had developed the double helix theory. Shortly after starting out as a research associate at UBC, I spent several weeks at the National Bureau of Standards in Washington, DC, working with Irwin Oppenheim. Irwin was sharing a house with a well-known microbiologist, Sidney Bernhard, and they had provided me with accommodation. One day, just before I was due to leave, Sidney told me that a friend of his would arrive during the night and would use the other bed in the room where I was sleeping. I would meet him the next morning at breakfast. His friend was called Watson and he had just done some interesting work in biology. Watson had come to consult with Bernhard concerning a decision he had to make and which they would discuss at breakfast, to which I was invited. I talked with Irwin before going to sleep, and he told me that there was a strong rumour that Watson would be nominated for the Nobel Prize. By the time I joined the breakfast group, they were well into the discussion. Watson had two job offers, one as a full professor at Indiana University, his alma mater, with generous research support. The other was at Harvard, and it carried no guarantee of tenure. They discussed all the arguments in favour of choosing Indiana, but in the end Watson went to Harvard.

I found the discussion very interesting because I had had to make a similar decision the previous year. I had agreed to accept a position at UBC as a research associate, and I was asked whether I would prefer to be considered for a position as assistant professor. I knew what the teaching load would be and I had no trouble deciding that I was better off with the research associateship, since it would enable me to launch my own research program instead of getting bogged down in all the preparatory work involved with teaching.

During my professional life, I've seen valuable contributions to the development of quantum physics, including those by Richard Feynman. He has also said some important things about how scientific knowledge is developed: "The way a field advances is often governed by someone who does introduce new ideas, however luckily, that stimulate other people to see things in a new manner…" Feynman himself showed in his PhD thesis that quantum radiation theory is an example of "action at a distance," and although the idea was controversial, his supervisor, John Wheeler, encouraged him to publish. The mathematical approach proposed by Feynman in this publication is now a well-established part of quantum mechanics, although there are still controversies about the interpretation of the theory.

Similarly, when physicists George Uhlenbeck and

Samuel Goudsmit were young students in Amsterdam, they realized that a certain kind of spectrum of magnetic systems had some characteristic wavelengths associated with them and that these could be interpreted as a manifestation of the fact that the electrons in the molecules and the atoms were spinning around. So they called it spin, "electron spin." When they shared this idea with their adviser, Paul Ehrenfest, he responded: "Well, I don't understand it and you probably don't understand it, so what've you got to lose? You should publish it."

Within a short time, this research was published in a journal, and Wolfgang Pauli, who was well respected for his important contributions to the field of quantum mechanics, made some devastating comments. He said that if you have spin, then the ratio of the magnetic moments should be twice as big or something like that. In fact, he had discouraged some young people in his own group from publishing similar research because he said they had to explain it first. As a result, Uhlenbech and Goudsmit got all the credit for the idea of electron spin, which is an important part of the theory behind nuclear magnetic resonance, just because Ehrenfest said: "What've you got to lose?" Pauli was a very good critic, but students were intimidated by his caustic and very critical remarks. Uhlenbech later wrote in a general article on the history of the field that he didn't have the slightest idea what Pauli meant by this factor of two, but he felt that Ehrenfest had given the right advice because the concept was very important. And just by bringing this concept forward, even without understanding it, they got credit for it. In my opinion, they should get credit for this idea, because science advances by increments. In other words, sharing a seminal new idea can take it beyond what you imagine because others have different intuitions and might take it in a direction that did not occur to you. I'm sure the same thing happens in art and music; when new concepts are introduced, they can be very fertile stimuli.

Another thing Feynman said that stuck with me was: "...and needless to say, lucky hazards play an equally conspicuous part in the history of scientific discovery." I hope you can see already that "lucky hazards" certainly played an important role in making me a physicist.

CHAPTER 2.

IT'S GOOD TO HAVE HEROES

As a kid in Montreal in the 1930s my identity, like other children's, was very strongly dependent on where I lived, and that meant not only the general neighbourhood but the specific block in which my house was located, i.e., an area of approximately one hundred by twenty metres. The character and culture of the next block was almost like a foreign country to me before I went to high school at about age twelve, in 1941. None of the families I knew when I was between the ages of five and fifteen owned their own houses. Families moved frequently, and there was an official moving day (May 1) on which it seemed that the furniture and other possessions of a large fraction of the flats were massed on the curb awaiting the moving vans.

The Bloom family were ethnic Jews from Europe, part of the wave of Jewish immigrants who arrived in Montreal between 1900 and 1950. After the immigration stop in Halifax, these immigrants reached Montreal by steamship or by train and many of them settled in an area defined roughly by Park Avenue on the west and St.

Denis Street on the east. The centre of this seam was, approximately, St. Lawrence Boulevard (also called Main Street). The western fringe of this strip was bordered by a "mountain" roughly 200 metres high (Mount Royal) and the eastern side by the commercial district of Montreal, which was well established by the francophonie.

After World War II, the balance of ethnic groups shifted: Southern European immigrants, mostly Greek and Spanish, began to move into the area parallel to Main Street that had previously been occupied mostly by immigrants from Eastern Europe. The Portuguese settled in the newly developed restaurant district east of Main Street between Prince Arthur and Rachel. In the area north of Mount Royal on Park Avenue, there developed a strong Greek community.

Later, many of the Eastern European Jews moved west of the mountain, to areas such as Côte St. Luc, though others remained near the original centres—especially those around synagogues—and maintained a strong focus of Jewish culture there. These shifts in population happened after I left Montreal, however, and from 1928 until my departure from Montreal as a graduate student in 1950, I lived in this seam of transition, in flats rented by my parents.

Although my sisters and I had no hand in selecting our parents, we realized from an early age that we were winners in God's throw of the dice. Our good fortune was made manifest when we celebrated our mother Leah's ninetieth birthday, not just because we may have inherited some of her "longevity genes" but because our mother demonstrated by example how to live with enjoyment and gusto while contributing to our collective improvement.

The ethnic diversity of our family is typical of Canadians from ethnic communities. My mother, Leah (née Ram), was born in Liverpool, England, in 1905, about five years after her parents arrived there from Poland, and her youngest brother, Louis, was born about seven years later. She also had four older brothers, born before her parents moved to Liverpool: Max (1893), Joe (1895), Harry (1897) and Sol (1899). Max and Joe had been sent to Montreal with relatives at the time her parents immigrated to England, and Leah met them for the first time when her brother Sol brought her and Louis to Canada in 1920, the year after her parents died.

My father, Israel ("Izzie") Bloom, was born in Novograd Volynsky (Ukraine) in 1900 and lived there until he immigrated to Canada with his family in 1913. He was the eldest, followed by his sisters, Tillie and Lilly, and then his brother Ben. It was the birth of a second son that ultimately led the family to emigrate, since if it had become known that he had a brother, Izzie would immediately have been conscripted for the tsar's army. Until the family was able to leave, Ben was kept hidden in the basement, and if he had to go out for any reason, he was dressed in girls' clothes.

I like the story of Leah and Izzie's meeting, as described in my mother's memoir. Apparently, my father approached her, offered her a bag of peanuts and a few moments later returned and asked: "May I have a couple of peanuts?" This led to a long walk while they shared the peanuts, then they went to see a movie and talked a blue streak.

When my mother returned home much later than expected that day, her sister-in-law asked, "Why are you so late?" Leah explained that she had met a young man, to which her sister-in-law replied: "That's fine, but next time bring him here and introduce him"—which she did. And from then on, for about four years, they got to know each other. They went to the movies and Izzie would tell her about the politics of the day—Marxism, of course—which he and most Russian immigrants his age would have adopted. Leah was only sixteen when they met, and she enjoyed learning what was behind the movement, finding the interplay of ideas very interesting and respecting him for his interest in and knowledge of political ideas. This kind of conversation obviously enriched her life.

Izzie felt he had an obligation to help his parents who were struggling to make a living from their small convenience store. His primary ambition was to become an engineering student at McGill, and he went to night school to build on his early education in Russia and to learn English. He had two major recreational interests, gymnastics and chess, which he was able to pursue through activities organized by the city. However, a source of frustration for him was that the equipment required for gymnastics could not be used during the winter and his search for suitable indoor facilities led to a legendary, though possibly apocryphal, story in our family.

As a teenager, Izzie found that indoor facilities for gymnastics were only available at the YMCA, the Young Men's Christian Association, but Jews were not eligible for membership in this club. This form of discrimination was common in the pre-WWII era. According to the story, Izzie applied for membership at the club and because of his Russian accent, gave his name as "Michael Romanov" and his religion as Russian Orthodox. A few days later, once the membership committee had reviewed the new applications for membership, Izzie returned to see the membership secretary who received him cordially but informed Izzie that, regrettably, Russian Orthodox people were not eligible for membership in the YMCA. When telling this story years later, Izzie could not contain his laughter as he remarked that the membership secretary did not even recognize that Michael Romanoff was the name of Russia's first tsar.

I have already said that when Izzie and Leah were courting, he was well read in modern philosophical writings and that he had read this literature in the Russian language. I know Izzie had very progressive political and philosophical ideas, but he became disillusioned with the Soviet Union before that attitude became fashionable. In 1971–72, I was on sabbatical leave in France with my wife and children, and when my parents came to visit us there, Izzie refused our invitation to visit Novograd, saying that nothing left in that part of the world was of any interest to him. It must have been extremely distressing to totally abandon his culture and first language, but he felt it necessary because of the direction Soviet politics had taken and the bad things he felt had happened to Jewish communities in his hometown. Nevertheless, Izzie's past as an intellectual non-conformist and liberal thinker manifested itself in the open and spirited manner in which ideas were constantly being tossed around in our home.

And though she lacked formal education beyond Grade 8, Leah was always reading and able to discuss books and ideas at a high level, so that my sisters and I were aware of a wide range of modern literature right from the start. We were (and remained) very active readers, probably due to her influence.

Every weekday, Monday through Friday, from about 12:15 to 1:00 p.m., we gathered for an extremely lively and harmonious family lunch throughout our early years in Montreal. I'm not sure how Izzie managed to get home every lunch hour from St. Catherine Street, where he was head cutter and designer in a ladies' coat factory for many years. When my sisters and I came home from school, a raucous and rapid exchange of news took place from that morning's activities, jokes, complaints and so forth. I recall Izzie always having at least one new joke—a sort of hobby that he took up more systematically in his retirement.

There was also a loud exchange of witty ideas and jokes around the kitchen table virtually every Sunday morning, between roughly 10:30 a.m. and noon. Leah's brothers Max, Joe and Louis, who were living in Montreal when we were growing up, dropped in to visit us regularly, often on Sunday mornings. Leah's other brothers, Sol and Harry, were living in England at that time. Sol and his wife, Dinah, had returned to Liverpool shortly after Leah and Louis arrived in Canada, though they did come back to Montreal with their two daughters soon after World War II ended. And I later met my Uncle Harry in December of 1954, when I took a trip to England soon after I began my post-doctoral work in Leiden in the Netherlands.

The Rams are a family of extroverts who really enjoy witty conversation, banter and repartee. This was true of all the Ram uncles and it is also characteristic of many of their children, my cousins. My guess, from talking to my mother, is that this agreeable wit originated with my maternal grandfather, Myer Ram. And from her memoir, I learned a bit more about this man who died in 1920 at the relatively young age of fifty-four. I'm really glad to have his name.

It is interesting to me to compare the personalities of the Rams and the Blooms, my heritage. The Blooms also enjoy banter and repartee, but theirs is mixed with an element of introversion not found in the Rams. I find it amusing to identify the odd mixture of these personality traits in myself, as well as in my sisters and our children.

My earliest memory of where we lived is the house at 4427B St. Dominique Street, which was on the third floor of a typical Montreal walk-up. A winding staircase outside the building led to the second floor, where a door opened to another staircase inside that reached to the third-floor flats. Our block was located between Marie-Anne Street, with its the little "Portugal Square," at the south end and Mount Royal Avenue, which lay all of 100 metres north. Several blocks east was a French-speaking quarter that was considered to be potentially dangerous for Jewish kids. To the west was more of the Jewish quarter, and then, crossing St. Laurent, Clark, St. Urbain and Esplanade, the playing fields on Fletcher's Field (now Jeanne-Mance Park) and the mighty Mount Royal. Our parents bragged that they had climbed "the mountain" many times while courting, an ascent made by only a small minority of Montrealers, and we were indeed impressed.

I have many pleasant memories of disconnected events and activities associated with my time on St. Dominique Street, and I remember my days being completely filled. As books passed through our living room, my mother read them all very quickly and I turned the pages of a lot of them, whether or not I actually read them. When the weather was bad, I would spend more time reading and I did learn to read before I started school.

Also during that time, my father used to take me along with him to the Rachel Market (one block east of Marie-Anne) on Sunday mornings to buy fresh vegetables directly from the French-Canadian farmers. (Years later, when I moved to Vancouver, I found myself making my own weekly visit to Granville Market on Sundays.) When we returned from those shopping trips, Izzie took great pleasure in assembling the fresh green vegetables and Montreal's wonderful rose tomatoes in artistic profusion on a large plate as the centrepiece of our Sunday lunch. He had a special knack for treating scallions: rubbing them vigorously with salt and crushing them with a fork made them sweet and amazingly tasty.

I also remember my parents eating each course of all their meals from a plate they shared. For many years, I thought that all parents had this custom and only later did I realize that mine had started to eat that way early in their marriage when they had very few dishes and they continued to do it as a manifestation of their love and the closeness of their relationship. Eventually, this custom became a source of friendly teasing within the family, which my parents accepted with good-natured equanimity.

From those days, I vividly recollect the milk being delivered each morning to our second-storey front door on St. Dominique Street. In the early years, the milkman used a horse-drawn conveyance and, in the winter, snow removers shovelled the snow into open wooden boxes set on horse-drawn sleds! Because the milk was left outside our door quite early each morning, it froze on most winter days. Those were the days before homogenized milk, and when the milk froze, the cream would rise to the top and push the cardboard cap up by several inches. I soon learned that this solid, cylindrical, top part went really well with cereal, and by getting up early each morning in the winter, I had a monopoly on this concentrated cream until my sisters caught on! I remember how sorry I was when we moved to 4248 St. Urbain Street in 1939 and, consequently, no longer had milk delivered by the Guaranteed Pure Milk Company.

I had liked the milkman and, as I recall, he came to collect his bill each Saturday morning. He would sit at the kitchen table for at least an hour, drinking tea and joking around with us while adding up the bill. He seemed like a friend of the family, and I continue to be surprised at how frequently this man's jovial, ruddy face appears in my memory. However, my memory of the milkman is suspect since when I talked with my mother about him many years later, she didn't remember him at all.

Outside the house, I participated in a wide range of

exciting street games with my friends who lived nearby. A version of street baseball, unique to our block, was played with a tennis ball as the only equipment. The rules were extremely complex, having been worked out over a long period of time to exploit all the ledges, nooks and crevices of the buildings on both sides of St. Dominique Street. The batters threw the ball against protrusions on the exterior wall of a building, which initiated an elaborate series of possible plays by the batting and fielding teams just like in regular baseball.

Buck buck was a game involving two teams and may have been responsible for back problems I experienced in later life. I believe that various versions of this game were widely played in Montreal. The four to six members of one team arranged themselves in a horse-like shape, each player bent over at the waist, back parallel to the ground and hands on the buttocks of the person in front. The members of the other team then ran across the street, one at a time, threw themselves high in the air and on to the backs of the awaiting team. The attackers had a limited time (about ten seconds) after all of them had "mounted" to break apart the horse-like structure and cause it to collapse while the "horses" tried to buck off their "mounts."

We also played street hockey in the small park at the corner of Marie-Anne Street or, more frequently, on our own street when it was covered by a hard layer of snow or ice. We played without skates but with pucks and hockey sticks, and these games, like all our street games, were played with great intensity, a minimum of equipment and no adult involvement whatsoever. Most hockey matches were pick-up games involving kids on our block, but we also played pre-arranged challenge matches against teams from different streets, e.g., St. Dominique versus Coloniale. By comparison, I feel sorry for today's ten-year-olds whose spontaneous games are squelched by the move to parent-organized Little Leagues, complex equipment and middle-of-the-night artificial-ice time on indoor rinks.

Up to the age of six or eight, all my sports and games were played on St. Dominique Street and involved other kids on the block, but once I grew older I spent more time on games that took place on Fletcher's Field. To get there, I had to cross two major streets, which required my parents' supervision. I'm sure this was the major reason for our move, a couple of years later, to St. Urbain Street, which was only one block away from Fletcher's Field, where many of the outdoor athletic activities of Baron Byng High School and the Young Men's Hebrew Association (YMHA) also took place.

My father had retained his interest in gymnastics and regularly went to the YMHA, which must have been constructed shortly after I was born, to work out using their equipment. When I was about nine years old, he began to take me along. After his workout, we had a swim together followed by a chocolate milkshake. I remember a number of occasions when, after the shower that followed his gymnastics workout, I was needed to hold open the door from the locker room to the pool while my father, walking on his hands, proceeded all the way to the diving board, up to the springboard and dove into the pool. After his swim, he would play several games of chess. He was an expert chess player and had played at a high club level before I was born. His old opponents would lie in wait for him and challenge him. I enjoyed these matches, since his opponents were seldom able to win.

The biggest effect of these visits to the YMHA was that when I was ten years old, I joined a new program called "Sports for Kids" that ran for about two hours each Sunday morning. We started with gymnastics involving equipment such as the horse, springboard, rings and parallel bars. Eventually we learned to relax and trust our leaders, the strong, stocky Tassy Singerman and the lithe, wiry Ike Potovsky, enough to vault into their arms. During the second part of our class, we played games such as badminton, volleyball and basketball. Tassy and Ike had the wisdom to work on both our individual and team skills.

I participated in enjoyable family activities too. We rode the streetcar to the lookout on Mount Royal, which involved walking for about a half-hour, and we enjoyed ice cream at the chalet near the lookout. We often walked to Lafontaine Park with its goose-shaped boat, and from time to time we took longer streetcar rides to St. Helen's Island, where the men could swim, or to Belmont Park, which was an amusement park.

When I was very young (perhaps seven or eight), I remember sitting on many successive summer nights at the periphery of a group of mostly older boys listening to one boy read a story he had written. This memory was triggered when I read of a similar group gathered around Franz Kafka when he was a boy in Prague. I wonder whether the narrator of the stories I listened to became a well-known writer, as there were several who came from our neighbourhood in that generation.

I should also mention some of the less pleasant incidents on St. Dominique Street, such as the ongoing conflicts with the "French guys" who lived nearby. On one occasion, an enormous masked mob of them invaded our neighbourhood carrying sticks and stones, and a nightmarish stone-throwing fight took place on Cérat, an alley next to our house; the "French guys" were finally routed by the "big (Jewish) guys" who were called from the pool hall located down the street. We were also frequently chased by these French guys as we made our way on foot through the French quarter from school to the free bleacher seats at the baseball park on De Lorimier Avenue, where the AAA-level Montreal Royals team played. Sometimes we caught the streetcar to the baseball park, if we managed to pick up a discarded transfer on the street or if we were given a ticket by our parents.

I was an avid collector of athletes' autographs as a young kid. One of my regrets is that, at some point while I was away in graduate school, my mother gave away my autograph book. I guess she felt that someone with a PhD in physics would no longer place value on such a collection. My collection must have made someone happy, as it included autographs from such luminaries as the great Jackie Robinson (before he broke into the major leagues with Brooklyn as its first black player), as well as other future stars such as "Pee Wee" Reese and "Duke" Snider.

Looking back, I appreciate my parents' judgment. In choosing our flat on St. Dominique Street, they had selected a location that allowed me to attend the "shiny new" Bancroft School just three blocks away rather than the dingy Mount Royal and Devonshire schools.

I remember entering Grade 1 in September 1934. My main concern each September, for the five years I was at Bancroft, was maintaining that my birthday was September 7 rather than December 7. In order to enroll me in school a year ahead of time, my parents had me tell this white lie and I was appreciative of their decision later in life. My Grade 1 teacher was Miss Morrison, and her primary activity was to teach reading and printing. Because I was younger than my classmates, I had trouble with printing but not with reading, probably because my mother had read so much with me.

My Grade 2 teacher, Miss Geller, focused more on the content of the stories. She was especially interested in promoting my own storytelling; in fact, she was so caught up in one of my stories that she kept the whole class late to hear the entire story. She continued to maintain her interest in my writing throughout that school year. There were two new programs in Grade 3, cursive writing and French language. I was conscious that I improved my understanding of English grammar through the study of French grammar. The class teacher seemed well suited to the formalities of the French language with her formal teaching tunic. My Grade 4 teacher, Miss Siminovitch, a lively woman, dressed more informally, like Miss Geller had. My Grade 5 teacher was a man, Mr. Smith. It was different having a man for a teacher because in his class learning seemed important.

I had to switch to Mount Royal School in Grade 6 because we moved to 4248 St. Urbain Street, right across the street from Baron Byng High School (BBHS), which I eventually attended. We remained there just a year, 1939, before we moved two blocks south, to 3933 St. Urbain. It was reputed that Mount Royal had a lot of "tough guys," and I had heard that it had a "tough teacher" to counter them. Miss Odell was said to be a savage strapper of mischievous boys, but I had no particular problems at that school. My teacher in Grade 6, Miss Zucker, was fascinated by choral speaking (not singing), and I established myself as a leading performer for solo passages. I remember being required to pipe up: "Play up, play up and play the game" in some British poem. I was also recognized for my story writing as I had been at Bancroft. My teacher for Grade 7 was Mr. Hole. His name went with his profession, which was to teach carpentry in addition to being a classroom teacher. He was strict, as was necessary for woodworking, and he had a gray handlebar moustache.

In the Montreal of my childhood, public schools were organized along religious lines and there were two school boards: Catholic and Protestant. There were also private schools, such as the Talmud Torah that were intended for Jewish students. Most Jewish children who attended public school were at Protestant schools, though many Jewish families in our neighbourhood also sent their sons to a Jewish school (cheder) after regular classes finished around 3:30 p.m. The cheders taught Hebrew and Jewish history and religion and, for boys under the age of thirteen, prepared them for their bar mitzvah. The religious ceremony, which marks the entry into manhood, includes a daunting ceremonial reading from the Torah in front of the entire congregation of a synagogue as part of the usual Saturday morning religious rites. Not to go through the bar mitzvah ritual was a minor disgrace in our community and provoked lively discussion and disbelief among our peers.

I believe that my sisters, Bernice and Dorothy, look back on their after-school Jewish education as having been interesting and rewarding but girls did not attend cheder. I can't say the same. At the age of about eleven, I was sent to a local cheder where I only lasted one day. During the very first lesson, one of the pupils misbehaved. I don't remember what the boy had done, but the rabbi decided to punish him. "Which pocket?" he asked. I didn't understand the meaning of this question but the boy did. "The left," he said and put out his left hand, whereupon the rabbi took a small leather strap out of his pocket and whacked the outstretched hand swiftly with two well-practised strokes. I didn't return to the cheder and my parents didn't press me to do so. I have a feeling that while the brutal, Old World, rabbinical educational methods provided me with a convenient excuse for ducking out of afterschool classes, I had also resented giving up my free time for the musty, sour smell of the cheder classroom.

Some months later, my father took me aside for a serious talk about preparation for my bar mitzvah. Izzie knew what he wanted me to do but he was totally noncoercive. He explained that if I wanted to be bar mitzvah at the usual age of thirteen, there was still time but I would have to start serious preparation soon. My parents had made some inquiries and found a highly recommended tutor, Mr. Z., who was prepared to give me private evening lessons once or twice a week. He would teach me to read Hebrew and focus on matters essential for my public performance in *shul* (synagogue). The decision was mine to make, he said, but I should keep in mind that I might, in future, regret not taking advantage of this final opportunity to advance beyond the threshold of manhood in the traditional manner. I accepted the offer. Perhaps it's appropriate to recall at this point that Izzie was a superb chess player (and strategist).

Mr. Z. was indeed a patient teacher. He put up with my occasionally not showing up for a lesson (at home) and knew exactly what was required for me to put on a good public display. By the time December 7, 1941, came about, I was able to sing the appropriate passage from the Torah in an impressive manner. He also wrote a speech for me to memorize and recite at the banquet before about 100 relatives and friends. The speech began (in Yiddish), "My beloved elders and friends, today I am a man!" It seemed to impress everyone but me. I had not really been consulted on the contents of the speech, and it made me extremely conscious of the fact that I had gone through the bar mitzvah ritual in the traditional manner primarily to please my parents and other relatives, especially my grandparents, and to maintain my status within the family. Once I had satisfied my family obligation, I discontinued my lessons with Mr. Z., which I now regret as I remember almost nothing of my studies of Jewish history and the Hebrew language.

Still, my father was right. Hypocritical though it may be, I would certainly have regretted not being bar mitzvah and I enjoyed the temporary eminence associated with the transition to manhood. Uncle Ben and his beautiful wife, Lillian, a former model, had come to Montreal all the way from Miami Beach, Florida, where he worked as a barman in a nightclub, just to celebrate my bar mitzvah with me. Ben had brought 100 US silver dollars as a gift to mark the occasion, and I was quite disgusted to learn that most of the money given as gifts to me, including his silver dollars, would have to be used to pay for the banquet. After all, it was held at Moishe's, the best steakhouse in Montreal (the world?), which was located on "the Main," two minutes' walk from our home.

A day or so after my bar mitzvah, my father took me aside for a serious discussion. It was clear that he was somewhat ill at ease. "Now that you are a man," he began, "you will be taking more responsibility for your life." I looked at him expectantly. "For example," he continued, "you now have a weekly allowance of fifty cents, which I propose to increase to one dollar to help you with your new responsibility. We could consider increasing it even more after a while." I expressed my deep appreciation of the confidence he had in me. Still, it was evident that our discussion was not yet finished. Izzie went on (I wish I could remember the exact words), "You know that men and women produce babies. Also, animals do things that have a similar result. Now that you're a man, we should, maybe, talk about it." I could see more or less where he was heading and was reluctant to follow him all the way. Though I didn't really know all that much about sex and had had absolutely no personal experience, I muttered something that succeeded in steering the conversation in a different direction. Izzie didn't give up completely on carrying out his fatherly responsibility on sex education, however. He returned to the subject when I started dating girls a few years later, but again I "headed him off at the pass." I regret not having been mature enough to allow my father to give me his advice on sexual matters. I wonder how he was planning to deal with this difficult subject.

Later in life, especially upon my "retirement" at age sixty-five, I reflected on the nature of transitions in the lives of men and women. In physics, we often try to understand phenomena by considering extreme cases. When it comes to transitions in the physical "state" of a system, we consider two extreme types of transitions called "sudden" and "adiabatic." In a "sudden" transition, the physical conditions change so quickly that it is imme-diately evident that a transition has taken place. In con-trast, in an "adiabatic" transition, the physical conditions change so gradually that they are imperceptible. My ten-tative conclusion is that when it comes to human transi-tions recognized by society, such as bar mitzvah or offi-cial retirement from work, the financial aspects are sud-den while the sexual and emotional aspects are adiabatic.

A short time after my bar mitzvah, my grandfather, Louis Bloom, died suddenly of a heart attack at the age of sixty-two. As the eldest grandchild, I remember always being treated with great affection but I don't feel as though I got to know my grandfather as a person. What I do recall is that he was a tall, severe-looking man with a very bald head. At the time of his death, he had owned a store selling soft drinks, cigarettes, candy bars and snacks in a small factory building in downtown Montreal. And as that business represented the only income for my grandmother, his widow, Sheine Rochel (Beautiful Rachel), she proposed that our family continue to run the business. My mother had helped her father-in-law from time to time, and in the end she took over the business and my grandmother came to live with us and took over the housekeeping. Eventually my father left the garment industry, and he and my mother owned a series of coffee shops in this factory area, which provided their income.

Around that time I entered Grade 8 at Baron Byng High School (BBHS), and unlike elementary school there were different teachers for each subject. Among my teachers was Mr. W.E. Jones, who taught physical education. Along with a number of other teachers in the school, he had immigrated to Canada from Britain after World War I. He had been a sergeant in the British army and spoke with a Cockney accent. Each year, he made an introductory speech to incoming students, pointing out that he was one of us, which could be determined from the reverse acronym of his name (WEJ). Author Mordecai Richler, who was a graduate of Baron Byng, used Mr. Jones as a character in *The Apprenticeship of Duddy Kravitz*, changing only his name, which appears as W.E.B. James. In fact, a number of my teachers are portrayed in Richler's book with different names but verbatim accounts of their remarks.

I remember the teachers at Baron Byng as being competent and experienced. Most had joined the school's teaching staff after World War I and they were beginning to reach retirement age in the 1940s when I attended. In class, we addressed them as "Master (name)" but outside of class, whether they knew it or not, we had a nickname for each teacher. For example, Mackinnon was "Mech," Calder was "Tuchus" and O.J. Lummis was "Yoss."

None of the teachers who taught French were native speakers, which in retrospect seems surprising. We took two French classes each year: writing, in which we studied French literature, and conversation, in which we practised speaking. I used to say that I learned to speak French from a Welshman and two Scots.

Mr. Lummis taught physics, but the only thing I remember from that experience is not from his class. He wore a hearing aid, and one day I played a nasty trick on him by modulating my voice for an unconscionably long time. He caught on to what I was doing and punished me by keeping me after school until I had carried out an assignment according to his direction. I was to measure the periods of simple and complex pendula, to establish the relationship between the period and length for several of them and to think of the significance of what I had done. By the time I finished the assignment around 6:00 p.m., I realized how serious he was as a teacher who wanted me to understand.

Most notable, among my high school student experiences, was singing in the choir. Mr. Herbert had been developing the choir for twenty years, and though singing in the choir was voluntary, most students participated and valued the experience. Mr. Herbert maintained choral discipline by threatening to expel anyone who did not give his or her attention to him when he asked for it. The choir definitely promoted good feeling among the students.

Our art teacher was Anne Savage, who was well recognized as an artist. Two of her paintings still hang in the Vancouver Museum. She was a good friend of A.Y. Jackson and the Group of Seven.

Although I participated in many activities at the high school, I became very active in athletics as a result of my early exposure to gymnastics and sports at the YMHA. The Y had an outstanding basketball coach, Moe Abramowitz, who decided to form a juvenile team to compete in a municipal basketball league. To recruit players, he attended some of our Sunday morning sessions looking for players who were under fifteen years of age and interested in playing in a league. That is how I got started in competitive basketball. The team was very successful, and we continued on to the Dominion of Canada juvenile (ages ten to fourteen) and junior (ages fifteen to eighteen) championship levels. At one point, we were the Eastern champions. My participation in basketball gave me an opportunity to travel to cities such as Windsor and St. Catharines, Ontario, where our pictures appeared in the local newspapers and we were greeted by local mayors and made to feel important.

Moe Abramowitz also gave me a piece of advice that has stuck with me. He said: "While you're learning, when you're early in your development of your understanding of how to do things, of how to be a good basketball player, select some people that you admire for their ability to succeed and try to emulate them." In my case, he sort of guided me into learning about how some of the small Jewish basketball players in New York City made a big impact by developing special skills that compensated for their size and gave them an advantage over other players.

That's obvious, I suppose, but he was really telling me, and the rest of the team, how to acquire a better understanding of the game and how to make our abilities count. In other words, pay attention to how others do things, go beyond the superficial. It's a lesson that's useful in science or art or any discipline. It's good to have heroes to look up to and learn from.

My hero in physics in my field is Ed Purcell. He's my spiritual "grandfather," because he was the supervisor of my supervisor. We use family words when talking about a particular line of researchers because there's a scientific culture associated with each group. Some groups of researchers remain productive and creative longer than any individual scientist in the group, which leads us to think in terms of a family of some kind.

However, back when I was in high school I was more focused on basketball than on physics. The excellent coaching we got from Moe at the Y greatly improved the calibre of our high school basketball team, since most of us played for both teams. The school acquired a new coach, Steve Armstrong, himself a basketball player who played in the city's Senior League, and with him we won the championship of the Protestant School Board when I was in Grades 11 and 12. Armstrong also initiated a playoff game between the winners of the Protestant and Catholic School Boards, and in my senior matriculation year, our team from Baron Byng topped our opponents from the Catholic School Commission by one point to become the Montreal high school basketball champions.

The fact that the game was won by one point on a shot I made in the last second of the game elicited a burst of enthusiasm from Coach Armstrong. He was certain that when I entered McGill, I would become a member of the varsity basketball team. That is, in fact, what happened and I found that I had a full schedule keeping up with my coursework and maintaining my position on the basketball team, which required as much study and practice as time would permit.

At Baron Byng High School, I played soccer when I was in Grade 11 and our team won all its games in the high school league, scoring a total of fifty-six goals over the ten-game series without having a single goal scored against us. At the time, the teachers at Baron Byng were opposed to football as a competitive high school sport because of the potential for injury, so we did not have a team. Recently developed awareness about the prevalence and long-term effects of concussion among high school football players indicates the wisdom of that decision, and I believe that the incidence of concussion should be reviewed for all contact sports.

I also joined a baseball team at the Y, which was coached by Niggy Rabin. I played shortstop, and also pitched. Intramural baseball games were almost always softball games, but I also played the more demanding hardball and while I was still in high school, I was one of the few nominated by my team for a tryout with the Montreal Royals, the AAA farm team for the Brooklyn Dodgers. Over 100 kids were at that tryout, which was not enough time to really show what we could do, and I was not selected for more professional training.

In high school I belonged to a group of friends that called ourselves the "Weasers." Some of my friends were

Lou Endman, Hy "Lefty" Berger, Murray Bronstein and Saul Karanofsky. It was as close as I ever came to participating in a gang, but the closest we came to breaking a law was sneaking into movies. At that time, many young people became adept at sneaking into movies because they were not allowed to buy a ticket. As a result of a couple of fires in the 1930s, for example the one at the Laurier Palace Theatre in 1927 where more than seventy children perished, the city was so shocked that it had ruled that children under sixteen not be allowed to enter cinemas. This law remained in effect throughout my adolescence, though the city seemed to overlook some movie houses, which undoubtedly provided bribes, such as the Midway and the Crystal Theatre near the corner of St. Catherine and St. Laurent, where cowboy pictures were shown.

As a teenager, if you wanted to see a movie and were prepared to pay for a ticket, you could go to Verdun, which was outside the Montreal municipality and therefore not bound by the same rules. You could also see a film at church or religious school, both of which received special permission to screen movies in spite of the fact that these venues were significantly more hazardous "fire traps" than the theatres. Another way to get into a movie was to wait at the exit of a theatre and enter while patrons were leaving the previous screening and before the door locked. It was not uncommon for more "customers" to be waiting at the exit than at the entrance!

Our friend Saul Karanofsky had never sneaked into a movie because he was afraid of being caught. We finally persuaded him to join us at Loew's Theatre at St. Catherine and Mansfield Avenue. It was the fanciest cinema in town and it showed Cecil B. DeMille movies. On this particular occasion, we were spotted sneaking in through the side fire-exit door. Although we discreetly made our way to seats, the managers called the police and the police carted us off to the precinct station. This was terrible for Saul. The man in charge was a French-speaking sergeant with a mischievous grin who said he might tell our parents about this incident, and if we were caught again, we would have to pay a fine. You could tell he didn't mean it. He interviewed us and pretended to take our names down. When he got to Saul, he asked in his thick French accent: "'ow you spell Saul?" We thought that was hilarious, but Saul was really worried.

My friends and I weren't always getting into mischief! We had been recruited to participate in a club program at the YMHA that was designed to produce well-rounded young men by sponsoring social, cultural and sports activities. There were three groups, and each group had a mentor provided by the Y, which also supplied a meeting room, the gymnasium and some money to pay invited speakers if needed. Some of the discussions were quite philosophical. For example, one speaker talked about Eastern religions and the Hindu view of reincarnation, which made me think about the origins of life and evolution. My group was called the "Cosmos Club" and we were in competition with the other groups. The club also encouraged social activities with women, and we had parties quite frequently, to which a roster of girls was invited, usually because they were attractive or because they were good dancers.

One of my friends, Lefty Berger, had attended Montreal High School before moving into the Baron Byng school region, and one of his classmates there was Oscar Peterson. Later Oscar played regularly at the Alberta Lounge, where he was discovered by a well-known New York jazz critic. The critic was in a taxi on his way to the Montreal airport when he heard a live radio program featuring Oscar Peterson and apparently told the taxi driver to go to the Alberta Lounge instead. Even after Oscar Peterson became famous, the Weasers were always welcome to attend his shows at the Lounge, and I often enjoyed his performances.

When school was out, my cousins Frank and Shirley, who lived in New York with their widowed mother, Auntie Tillie, frequently spent summers with us. Frank and I got along very well and we had numerous adventures. On one occasion, we encountered a bear in the forested hills above the house we had rented one summer in Shawbridge, a small town north of Montreal. The bear was about twenty feet away, with a forest on the left and a hill on the right. We did the right thing—we pretended we had not seen it—and the bear did the same thing with respect to us; it ambled off into the forest.

In later years, our families switched the summer escape from Montreal to Woodlands, a community located twenty-five kilometres southwest of Montreal on Lake St. Louis, because my father was interested in fishing. It was an easy commute by train or bus, and the fishing was very good. We were able to rent a large house from a farmer, Monsieur Dupont, who moved his own family, a wife and two small children, into a smaller summer house on the property. The farm was typical of the *habi-*

tant, a long and thin plot about a mile long and 300 feet wide with frontage on the lake. Frank and I offered to help Monsieur Dupont in his agricultural activities, and he accepted our offer. We enjoyed collecting and processing hay and harvesting other vegetables. We went to call the cows in for milking, and we were taught how to milk a cow, but we never reached the speed needed to compete with Monsieur Dupont. He could milk all four cows in less time than it took us to do one. He would squirt us with the milk as it was coming out.

Up to Grade 11, I had had very little social life involving girls. However, when I was about to graduate from Grade 11, Shirley (Cookie) Nirenberg invited me to be her escort to the party held by her class. At Baron Byng, the girls and boys were in separate classes, and in Grade 11 the girls' classes held parties to celebrate graduation. I had got to know Cookie because she was on the girls' basketball team at the high school, and earlier that year she and another member of the team, Ellen Steinberg, had invited me and a few others to help their team improve their play. I had accepted their invitation to coach the team but it hadn't proven to be useful as girls' and boys' basketball had very different rules. In spite of good intentions, I wasn't able to improve the girls' play. However, since girls and boys were in different classes, I was happy for the social contact with the girls. Cookie was a very attractive girl with high colour and red cheeks, and I accepted her invitation, went to the party and enjoyed her company. I was sixteen years of age and typical parties of that era featured dance music of several types: big band, fast songs for jitterbug dancing, and slow romantic tunes for close dancing. This experience opened doors for me, and I was never again shy with girls.

I continued to see Cookie from time to time after graduation, but we were both very busy. I believe she went on to McGill and studied first-year science at the Dawson College campus during the following year while I remained in the Senior Matriculation Program at high school. In general, those I knew who went to Dawson College seem to have enjoyed it and, eventually, Cookie became a biologist.

Ellen was a year younger than Cookie and me, and beginning in Grade 12 I began to see her regularly. We started out at McGill, on the Montreal campus, the same year. She went on to complete the teacher certification program at Macdonald College in Ste. Anne de Bellevue, but she had always been interested in the theatre. Later, she developed a successful career that combined her interest in performance with her background in education by becoming "Miss Ellen" in the TV program *Romper Room* for children. I must have gone out with Ellen for four or five years, and in the summer of 1948, we were both counsellors at Camp Escobar in the Laurentian Mountains north of Montreal, where there was an emphasis on sports and wilderness experience. I was a success as a counsellor because my technique for getting the boys to settle down each night was to tell stories that I based on my reading of books like *The Count of Monte Cristo*. To my unexpected delight, I was able to maintain the respect of my fellow counsellors by the success of my storytelling for the entire summer.

We had one day off each week, and Ellen and I enjoyed

being able to go off and practise on our own what we were learning about the wilderness at the camp. However, the following summer, when I was able to get a summer job at Chalk River, Ontario, and Ellen realized that I was making plans to do a PhD program at a university in the United States—a four-year commitment—she recognized that I would not be available for marriage for another four years. She told me that she was not prepared to wait that long, and she suggested that we remain friends but that we cancel the tacit understanding that we were engaged. My reaction was very strange and unexpected to me: when I left her apartment that evening I felt a sense of freedom, and as I walked home I was singing and dancing in the street.

We continued to correspond until Christmas of 1950, although the letters became more infrequent. My last communication to her, from Urbana, Illinois, was a postcard with the Greek letter for Nu on it. In Yiddish, when you say *nu*, you're asking what is going on. It was then that I learned that Ellen had married her neighbourhood friend and was happy to have joined him in Zurich, where he was enrolled in a medical program. I later heard from a mutual friend that her husband had obtained an internship in Cincinnati, Ohio. As far as I know, they had a happy marriage.

CHAPTER 3.

PHYSICS: THE ULTIMATE THRILL

After I completed the Senior Matriculation Program at Baron Byng, I entered the Joint Honours Program in Mathematics and Physics at McGill in September 1946 along with about thirty other students. These honours programs were considered to be tough courses and only selected students were permitted to enrol in them.

Before entering this program, I didn't really know what physics was. Perhaps more importantly, that first year at McGill I discovered the thrill of mathematics. I was taking a calculus course with Dr. Sullivan and I was worried that I would fail. But over the Christmas break I wrestled with the problems and finally began to experience a breakthrough in my understanding. This experience of succeeding "under my own steam" was really pivotal in developing my creative skill as a scientist, and in the short term it fostered a confidence that I hadn't had previously. By the time I got through the second-year science program, I realized that I had fun solving these problems—that I liked the feeling that accompanied moments when I suddenly realized "aha, that's how it works"—as

I had experienced when preparing for Sullivan's exams. That's the feeling that swung me over to science. Before that, I was just having too much fun playing sports and reading books to contemplate anything else.

Sullivan's style of teaching was unorthodox. Among the students were several related to well-known scientists and academics, including the son of the president of the National Research Council at the time, E.W.R. Steacie; the son of the chairman of McGill's Department of Chemistry, Otto Maass; and the younger brother of a well-established professor of mathematics at McGill, Edward Rosenthall. Sullivan would clearly write the mathematical development he was presenting on the blackboard, he would discuss the connections between different aspects of the various lemmas and theorems, and then he would say: "Check?" If a student responded: "Check," Sullivan might go on or he might call upon that student to explain the presentation. If he got no response, he would use his class list and call on a student by name to tell what he was having trouble understanding. Then he would call on other students to explain it to the first student. At the beginning of the term he would call by name one of the relatives of the famous people, but as the term went on he would call on others as well. Sometimes he would ask several students questions and discover that the whole class didn't understand the presentation. His way of teaching inspired us to come to class well prepared.

Much later, I read an essay written by the famous French mathematician Henri Poincaré in which he described a period of hard and apparently fruitless effort to solve a problem. He took a break to join a geological expedition, and he wrote that as he was stepping on a bus, he made one of the most important breakthroughs of his life. The solution came to him out of nowhere and was accompanied by a feeling of perfect certainty as to its correctness. Poincaré did not claim that this was a miraculous incident. Indeed, he believed that we can solve problems when we are not consciously thinking about them. This idea of mathematical creativity resonated with me because of that experience in Sullivan's calculus course.

Years later, in 1958, I was invited to participate in a panel discussion in Parksville, BC, about creativity. The other speakers included a chemical engineer, the chair of the creative writing department, the head of the architecture group at the University of British Columbia, an English teacher, and several others. About 100 people sat in the audience, more than half were students, and the atmosphere in the room was informal. Most of the speakers addressed a variety of philosophical issues, none of which involved creativity, in my opinion. In contrast, I talked about Poincaré's essay, about the flash of insight you can get and about how that's what I liked about mathematics. I continued that although we do not know how to define creativity quantitatively, we can often agree that in any given field some people are more creative than others. Then I told them that most likely creativity comes from two factors: one is *energy* and the other is *experience*. And I postulated that the psychic energy of a person after birth generally decreases rapidly with time. However, the number of experiences a person has increases over time. I whipped up the formula:

creativity = energy x experience

One goes down with time, the other goes up. If you plot this kind of function, it will have a maximum like what is shown.

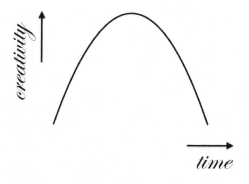

I told the audience that I felt I could only test this theory on myself, and so I went back to my elementary school and high school teachers and they agreed that my postulation sounded about right. I asked my mother and close friends, and they said that I probably had maximum creativity at a negative time—that negative time being before I was born. I went back to my mother to discuss this idea with her further and I decided it was okay because it showed I had creative energy as a fetus.

After the conference, I was besieged by students wanting to know where I had published this formula. I did not tell them that I had just made it up. I just said it had not been published. However, I believe that in the academic world we do not actually know how to teach people to be creative. It gave me pleasure to tease the other speakers—for example, I said that most literary criticism does not involve creativity—and they took it in good spirit, some saying they would do better next time. A few weeks later, at UBC, I was invited to repeat my talk at a series of noon-hour lectures with the title "My Last Lecture," and again I had a good response.

However, that was in the future. The physics courses I took in my first year at McGill—classical mechanics from Ferdinand Terroux, electricity and magnetism from Horace Watson, heat and thermodynamics from Norman Shaw (head of the physics department)—all used quite elementary mathematics. The following year, the mathematics courses provided the kind of background that was important to the physics courses that followed. What was positive about the physics courses that first year was the fact that we had great contact with the research tradition that originated in the Cavendish Lab at the University of Cambridge in the UK. The work for which Ernest Rutherford had won the Nobel Prize in Chemistry had taken place at McGill during the first decade of the twentieth century, and the equipment he had used was still there. It was used to create the Rutherford Museum, of which Terroux was the proud curator. This equipment could no longer be used for scientific research, however, because of radioactive contamination.

In my third and fourth years at McGill, Phil Wallace had a big influence on me. Looking back, I can say now that he was my main mentor at McGill. Since the McGill physics department had no theoretical physicists (a legacy of Rutherford's time as chair), Phil Wallace was appointed to the mathematics department and though the courses he taught in the Joint Honours Program were identified as mathematics courses, what he taught was actually theoretical physics. McGill still claimed a solid reputation in modern physics but this was due to Rutherford's research in radioactivity and atomic structure using the scattering of alpha particles.

Phil Wallace taught a more advanced classical mechanics course in third year, based on the text by J.L. Synge and B.A. Griffith; and in fourth year he taught a course in mathematical methods in physics. His presentations were clear and understandable and exciting because he was showing us what was actually happening in physics at the time. John Stuart Foster gave ten lectures at the end of this course, and all of us in the honours program found them incomprehensible. He seemed to feel that there was a lack of insight in the theoretical approaches whereas Wallace made us feel optimistic about the use of theory in the discoveries being made in physics. I was thrilled and excited about these new ideas and was inspired to take as many courses as I could in theoretical physics. I took Wallace's course in quantum mechanics, using the text by Leonard Schiff, in my master's program. This was an excellent text in its day, but David Bohm soon wrote a book that argued you couldn't have a self-consistent theory of quantum mechanics in which the uncertainties in the quantum variables were eliminated.

The following year I took a course with Dave Jackson on electromagnetic theory, which was designed for two semesters, but which our group completed in one. It was based on the advances that had been made leading up to the theory of quantum electrodynamics. I also had a sophisticated course in statistical mechanics from Ted Morris, who had recently obtained his PhD from the University of Toronto and who had been appointed as assistant professor in the Department of Mathematics.

When I went on to the University of Illinois for my own doctorate program, I got full credit for the courses I had taken with Wallace, Jackson and Morris, as these were considered equivalent to Illinois's PhD courses. What Jackson taught was the most important post-war graduate-level course in physics because it presented evolving semi-classical theories.

I first learned about nuclear magnetic resonance (NMR) in 1948, when I was in the final year of my bachelor of science program. I had been attending, whenever possible, the regular weekly colloquia of the McGill Physical Society. Most science departments or institutes offer seminars for the benefit of their students and faculty, and the speaker is usually advised to direct the introduction to beginning graduate students and the frontier part to advanced graduate students and faculty. Looking back, I see the main benefit of attending such seminars regularly is cumulative in that over time you start to develop a feeling for the frontiers and boundaries of the field. When I later organized weekly seminars for the Department of Physics at UBC, I encouraged my undergraduate and graduate students and faculty in my own and related departments to attend them, with good results. Once in a while, however, a new and really bright idea can capture your imagination and influence almost all of your future work. Such was the effect on me of a lecture presented by Karl K. Darrow in late November or early December

1948. The title of the lecture was something like: "The Discovery of Nuclear Magnetic Resonance (NMR)."

Darrow was very well known in the American physics community, though not as a researcher but as secretary of the American Physical Society, a position he held for nearly thirty years. His main job was at Bell Laboratories, where he kept the researchers informed about recent scientific developments of importance. He had selected NMR as a prime example and he was absolutely correct.

After the seminar, I went to the reading room to continue preparing for the Christmas examinations. I noticed, in the gloaming of late afternoon Montreal in December, the profile of one of my professors, John S. Foster, director of the McGill Radiation Laboratory. He had also been at the seminar, and I intercepted him while he was on his way to the radiation lab. We talked about what an interesting seminar it had been, and I told him that I was interested in Darrow's remark that someone was setting up an NMR experiment in the lab. I explained that when I finished my bachelor's degree, I was planning to do a master's study and I was looking for a thesis project. The NMR project was very interesting to me, and I wondered if there might be an opening for me there. Foster reacted enthusiastically to this proposal. The PhD student involved was Don Hunten, who had had experience in the design and construction of the McGill cyclotron and had satisfied all his course requirements for the doctorate. He had decided to redirect his project to explore nuclear physics applications of NMR. He needed help to develop the NMR spectrometer, and Foster felt he would be a very good supervisor of someone with my background. Foster suggested that I visit the radiation lab the next day and that he would introduce me to Hunten.

When I showed up at 9:00 a.m., Foster was waiting for me in his office and we went to the machine shop where Don Hunten was standing in front of a slowly turning lathe and guiding a copper wire on to a coil former mounted on the lathe. Don was wearing thick gloves, and he made some jokes about the set-up being an efficient way of reducing the number of fingers on the hands of expert machinists fond of cracking jokes. In fact, Hunten was dealing with the problem of constructing a radio station with a transmitter *and* a receiver. The transmitter, a variable frequency signal generator, could be purchased "off the shelf" anywhere in the world. The receiver, an instrument capable of measuring nuclear magnetic dipole moment precession frequencies, had to be constructed to be able to efficiently receive the needed frequencies. For proton NMR, the receiver is tuned to the transmitter by varying a large magnetic field applied externally to match the proton precession frequency.

Before attending the seminar, I knew nothing about NMR. I did not know that C.J. Gorter, a well-known Dutch low-temperature physicist and director of the famous low-temperature Kamerlingh Onnes (KO) Laboratory, had made a serious attempt to detect the NMR signal. This attempt failed for reasons that were not clear at that time. The fact that Holland was an occupied country in 1943 when the best attempt was made must have made it difficult to carry out delicate experiments. I could not have foreseen that I would end up doing post-doctoral research at that laboratory.

When I started working in NMR in my final undergraduate year at McGill, 1949, Don Hunten and I took a trip to Harvard University for perhaps three days to see Edward Purcell's equipment. Purcell had received the Nobel Prize for his work on NMR that year. Don's wife joined us, and we were able to stay at the Cambridge residence of my fraternity. We phoned Purcell before leaving Montreal and asked if he could spare a couple of hours for us. He was very warm and said that he would be at Harvard Yard that day supervising an undergraduate laboratory measuring the intensity of electromagnetic radiation but that he would be available for a couple of hours. He showed us not only the NMR equipment but he gave us preprints of his unpublished work, including a paper on NMR. This was a groundbreaking paper by Herbert Gutowsky, George Kistiakowsky, George Pake and Purcell about previously unmeasured dipolar broadening in an NMR signal. It was difficult to read but it gave me an appreciation for the way he was able to frame the questions differently.

In the last year of my undergraduate program, I became aware of the possibility of getting a summer job in which I could make use of what I was learning. Up until then, I'd had summer jobs collecting bills for the CPR Telegraph Company (1947) and working at my parents' restaurant and as a counsellor at Camp Escobar, a summer camp for kids (1948). When I looked at all the job possibilities, one of the two most interesting ones included a geophysics program to measure the Earth's magnetic field in the far north of Canada. That seemed like a very adventurous way of spending the summer and would expose me to an important area of applied physics, earth sciences, and I applied for the job. The chairman of the selection committee was C.S. Beals, a distinguished scientist who held the honorific title of "Dominion Astronomer" (Canada was still a "dominion" in 1949) and who was the director of a telescope located in Ottawa where he had his home as well.

While filling out the application forms, I realized that I was going to be in Ottawa before the application deadline to play basketball with the McGill team against Carleton University. So I wrote to Beals and asked whether I could visit him on that day in March to find out more about the job. He invited me to have tea at his home. When I arrived, he was having a small garden party and I was told that the Dominion Astronomer would meet with me after some of the other guests had left. He was a very distinguished-looking man with white hair, and I noticed that he was sitting by himself for a while looking at documents from time to time. He caught my eye and smiled, and I assumed that he was looking at my application form. Indeed, when I came to sit at his table, my photograph was in the document that was open before him. Beals said that he was interested to read in my application form that my father came from Poland. I was embarrassed because I felt I had lied, since when I had asked Izzie whether the town where he was born was Russian or Ukrainian, he had said it was sometimes Polish as well. Beals commented that he could picture my head shape as being Polish. This remark concerned me for a while, but the interview went very well. Beals described the nature of the work in the far north and hinted that it was likely that my application would be successful and that I would enjoy leading the life of a geophysicist for a summer.

Reflecting on my visit with the Dominion Astronomer after I returned to Montreal, I was impressed by Dr. Beals's humanism and his being relaxed and cordial about a visit with an undergraduate student that took up a good part of his afternoon. I have since learned that leaders in the creative arts and sciences usually enjoy talking to students, the younger the better, as long as they sense genuine curiosity. It is useful to appreciate that experienced workers treasure their contact with neophytes in the field because they know they can learn just as much from the student as the student learns from them.

I had applied for summer jobs in December 1948 in order to meet the deadline for applications. If all went well, I would obtain my bachelor's degree at the end of that summer and my plan was to work for the summer and then return to McGill in September to begin my master's. I wanted to decide on a research program for my master's before leaving for my summer job at the beginning of May. By the time of my interview with Dr. Beals, I had come to the conclusion that I would rather learn about nuclear physics than geophysics. I felt that I had to decide whether I should immediately accept the offer of doing geophysics in the far north or whether I should explore the possibility of a summer job at the Atomic Energy Commission Laboratory (AECL) in Chalk River.

I telephoned the office at AECL that was in charge of summer students and explained my problem to the secretary who answered the phone. I had submitted an application to AECL but had not heard from the agency, and

I wanted to know whether or not I stood a chance of getting a job there. She understood immediately and said that I had called at just the right time. The chairman of the selection committee responsible for summer student appointments was standing beside her. Dr. Watson was the head of the theoretical physics division of AECL and he picked up the telephone. He said that he was looking at the final list of successful summer student applicants... and I was on it. Dr. Watson added, "The only missing information is the RCMP security check, so I anticipate meeting you in Chalk River in early May."

My mood was a mixture of anticipation and apprehension: anticipation because I was beginning to appreciate the high quality of the neutron research at Chalk River, research being carried out with the largest neutron flux in the world, and apprehension because I was aware of the increasing intensity of the Cold War, especially in the US. I began to wonder if I might be considered a security risk because I lived in Cartier, the only constituency in Canada that had (in 1943) elected a communist member of Parliament. In that election, Fred Rose received 43 per cent of the votes. It seemed unlikely, as I had been told the summer jobs at Chalk River were not sensitive and did not require a high level of security clearance.

As it turned out, our next-door neighbour was approached by a member of the Royal Canadian Mounted Police (RCMP). Picture, if you can, the RCMP officer in his bright red jacket walking up the external staircase leading to the second floor, then opening the door to the internal staircase that led to the third-floor flat. It was such an unusual and incongruous sight that passersby and neighbours would probably have expected him to break out into a Broadway musical song. His visit would certainly have attracted a lot of attention. The officer would then have rung the bell to the third-floor flat and our neighbour would have pulled the string that opened the latch on the door leading upstairs. As he did so, my neighbour shouted down the stairs, "Who are you and what do you want?" The RCMP officer replied, "I am Corporal Smith of the RCMP, and we are authorized to investigate security matters with respect to employees of the government. I can show you my ID if you wish. I have a simple question to ask you: 'Can you tell me whether Myer Bloom is a communist?'" My neighbour replied, "I don't know whether Myer Bloom is a communist and if I knew I wouldn't tell you. When you leave, please close the door!" Ironically, my neighbour was known to be a communist and I looked upon this whole episode as humorous.

I arrived in Chalk River during the first week of May 1949, looking forward to doing research in this famous laboratory and working on a problem in the most exciting of fields (in my naive opinion in 1949), nuclear physics. The lab had been set up during World War II as part of the Allied effort to develop the atomic bomb. At the same time, a "company town," Deep River, was built about ten kilometres to the west so the area in which the laboratory was located could be isolated, since not enough was known about the safety requirements with large neutron reactors (which is still the case). At that time, a fleet of buses transported the entire workforce of several thousand people back and forth between Deep

River and Chalk River and made it possible to overcome the disadvantage of geographical isolation. Such a modern, high-level research organization needed a well-educated, highly professional workforce, and the manner in which recreational activities had sprung up in Deep River had been helpful in attracting the type of technologically trained workers required at AECL. In fact, one of the administrators was very interested in sports and would hire, among the non-technical staff, people who were good athletes. We had a baseball team that was good enough to play in a semi-professional baseball league, and the players had lots of fun making short trips to play against teams from towns such as Petawawa and Pembroke. At one of the relaxed beer parties after the games, I acquired a girlfriend, the daughter of that administrator. She was the mother of a girl with spina bifida, and I admired the way she handled the girl's problems and I enjoyed the small town games, such as cribbage, that we played. And she needed someone to talk to and found more fundamental things to talk about with me than with other members of the club.

We were about twenty-five summer students that year, housed in a single dormitory building with two students in each room. We came from all regions of Canada and most of us were graduate students at an intense stage in our commitment to the study of physics. It didn't take long for us to become a lively group, interested in the variety of experiments and theory that we were learning at Chalk River, and only a few days passed before we organized an after-dinner seminar series in which we told each other how we were going to spend the summer.

I found that most of the projects had already been assigned to students who had arrived before me or who were returning for a second summer and were planning to complete the project they had started the previous summer. A few students had made arrangements through their PhD supervisors at their home universities to learn something important for their own theses. Among the few remaining projects, I was particularly interested in neutron scattering, a newly developed technique for exploring atomic structure, which was directed by Don Hurst. I was impressed by the fact he suggested that I not try to do a complete research project in one summer but learn several of the important experimental techniques crucial in the study of neutron scattering, such as neutron capture. One of the most important things I worked on was the use of boron trifluoride gas counters, into which a beam of neutrons was directed. The boron isotopes gave rise to the nuclear reaction where alpha particles result from absorbed neutrons. Dick Fowler, a permanent member of the research group at Chalk River, was a world leader in the measurement of the energy and momentum of neutrons in neutron beams, and I spent more than a month working with him.

Another important technique was Bragg scattering of neutrons. Don Hurst suggested that I work with Trudi Goldschmidt, a post-doctoral fellow who had recently joined AECL. She used Bragg scattering to determine crystalline properties and was working on the crystal structure of ammonium chloride solids. Trudi, who was actually a chemist, had worked with a Nobel Prize–winning crystallographer in Britain using x-ray diffraction for her PhD, and I helped her to develop numerical techniques for neutron scattering in the study of ammonium chloride. I worked with her for almost half the summer. In addition to supervising my work, she became a good friend. Life was always lively when Trudi was around. I told Trudi about my feeling that nuclear physics was the most important branch of physics and that I planned to work towards a doctorate in that area after completing my master's in 1950. Trudi was in agreement with me and said, in her usual forceful manner, "Kid, you should do your PhD studies at the University of Illinois and make sure that you work with the best nuclear physicist in the world, Maurice Goldhaber!"

I satisfied the McGill requirements for the bachelor's of science in May 1949 and I did the final work on the research for my master's of science degree between September 1949 and May 1950. When I returned to Chalk River for a second summer in 1950, Don Hurst had a completely new project for me that made use of the neutron scattering study I had done the previous summer but that gave me the opportunity to work independently. By the end of the summer, I had built a piece of apparatus to detect resonant scattering of slow neutrons by cadmium. The ability to detect this kind of scattering was important because it is accompanied by resonant absorption, which means that very few neutrons actually escape from the scattering material.

The neutron source at Chalk River was more intense than any other source at that time. Yet, when I completed my preliminary study I found that the intensity of the scattered beam was much weaker than I had anticipated.

We could see how to improve the outcome by making changes in the geometry of the scattering chamber but time was running out since I was scheduled to leave for the University of Illinois to begin my PhD program. Don Hurst was expecting the arrival of a new research scientist, Bert Brockhouse, who had written his PhD dissertation at the University of Toronto on ferromagnetic solids, and Bert arrived a couple of days before I left. I showed Bert what I had been working on, and he continued the research. Eventually he developed the triple-axis spectrometer and was awarded a Nobel Prize for this work. When this happened, I was very proud of having taught Bert to use the equipment I had developed.

I had applied for admission to PhD programs at several American universities and was accepted by the University of Illinois in Urbana, which had been my first choice because of Trudi's advice. My program was scheduled to begin on September 1, 1950, and I had been told there would be no problem in obtaining a student visa so that I could earn money from fellowships or research assistantships. However, when I went to the US consulate in July to obtain my visa, things were not so straightforward. I went through the formalities and everything seemed to be in order. By mid-morning, I was standing in front of the vice-consul about to swear that I would not try to overthrow the US government by force when he interrupted the proceedings and remarked, "I see that you wrote for this appointment from Chalk River, Ontario. Are you working at the AECL laboratory? In that case, you'll require a clearance before you qualify for a visa. We have just received a ruling to that effect."

I tried to argue with the vice-consul about his ruling. I pointed out that the RCMP had cleared me for my summer job at Chalk River, which involved only non-sensitive projects. The vice-consul felt that clearance would take only a short time and that "by the time the boys in Washington complete their job, you'll be clean as a sheet." His prediction that my clearance would go quickly turned out to be wrong, and I was still waiting for it at the end of August. I then decided to risk travelling to Urbana, Illinois, by train in order to register as a graduate student on campus. When questioned on the train by the immigration officials, I pretended to be a tourist rather than a graduate student planning to register for school in the US. I already had a place to live. A fellow student, Martin Boloten, from my graduating class at McGill had also decided to seek his PhD degree at University of Illinois in Urbana. When Martin discovered how similar our programs were, he invited me to share a room with him in the home of a music professor, Wolfgang Kuhn; his wife, Mary; and their three children. I could not have predicted that this quiet home would provide safe haven for Martin and me for three turbulent years surviving a tough PhD program.

CHAPTER 4.

MORE "LUCKY HAZARDS" AT ILLINOIS

I had gone to Urbana specifically to work with Maurice Goldhaber, but when I arrived neither he nor the department chairman, Professor Francis Wheeler Loomis, were on campus. I talked with the associate chairman, Gerry Almy, and he told me that Loomis was gone for a few weeks but that Goldhaber had moved permanently to become head of the Brookhaven National Laboratory on Long Island, New York. Almy said: "I guess Goldhaber didn't know you were coming." However, a program had been set up for me with the approval of the department. I was registered for a course called Kinetic Theory of Gases with Robert Maurer, and Directed Studies in NMR, which was supervised by Charlie Slichter. At that time, Slichter was an instructor in the physics department but he rose in rank very quickly and became a full professor before I graduated.

My work at the University of Illinois at this point was unofficial, since I still did not have the necessary documentation to be a student in the US. I found I was able to handle the coursework on my own and I returned to

Montreal in early October to see what I could do about getting the clearance. In mid-October I returned to Urbana without my clearance. After this, the department turned to the associate dean of graduate studies, who wrote a letter to Washington, and towards the end of November I returned to Montreal and obtained the official documents for my visa.

The graduate program at the University of Illinois was quite archaic in that before PhD students could do any research, there were qualifying exams, pre-preliminary exams and a preliminary exam to be taken. As a consequence, most incoming students spent one to two years in rigorous coursework before considering the research problem. The physics graduate students at University of Illinois were a very high-level group, including the best students from international and prestigious US undergraduate institutions as well as many students from small Illinois state colleges (the state government had ruled that graduates of Illinois schools with good marks must be admitted to graduate programs at the state university.) The examination system was a method of efficiently identifying students who were not qualified for the program.

Students without the required background were given a year to fill in their knowledge gaps before sitting the exams, and we could choose the subject in which to show that we had the necessary undergraduate experience. These included subjects such as mechanics, thermodynamics and optics. It had been explicitly stated that it should not be necessary to study for these exams, and I announced to my fellow students that I would not. I took the written exams before Christmas, but it was also necessary to pass an oral exam in one of the subjects and I chose optics. This was the qualifying exam that I failed: I was asked a tricky question regarding polarized light, my mind went blank and I could not even write down Maxwell's equations.

I had received a letter from the Province of Quebec letting me know that I had been awarded a two-year travelling fellowship, so I was free to study anywhere. I told Charlie Slichter, who became my research supervisor, that since I had failed the exam I would leave Urbana and go to Oxford. He replied that the committee had already established that I was qualified because of the work I had done at the undergraduate and master's levels, but that the professors wanted me to take the qualifying exams seriously. I was then given an oral exam in kinetic theory of gases, which I passed. The committee accepted that this result established that I was competent to do research at the PhD level.

I don't believe we really know how to assess a person's potential for doing creative research. At Illinois I found myself attacking the method used to assess research potential while my research adviser, Slichter, defended the physics department's policy on the qualifying examinations. I discussed this matter with Slichter when I saw him about twenty years later, and he confessed that he had found an inverse correlation between success in research and marks on exams. I have concluded that people use intuitive observations about the potential of individual students to do creative work and trust their judgment when it differs from the test results. We don't know how to teach reliable intuition in research or how to recognize this capacity in other people.

I had not had a good nuclear physics course at McGill, but I decided to take a graduate course in the subject, given by John Blatt. It was considered to be very demanding, and only four students—Martin Boloten, Al Redfield, Ken Teegarden and me—registered for credit that term. I remember spending the Christmas break working on a term paper on the alpha particle model of the nucleus. This was a very good topic because it was so broad, and Blatt was very pleased with my 100-page paper and said that he had learned a lot from it. I had approached this assignment seriously because I felt the need to improve my reputation after failing the exam. Blatt later told me that my essay had earned the top marks of the four students.

Ken had received a new car from his parents when he passed the qualifying exams, and I bought his old car for about $100. This was an Oldsmobile, the first car that was built with an automatic transmission. Later models had fluid coupling in the transmission, but this one involved bands that shifted gears mechanically and it made jingle-jangle noises whether I was driving fast or slow. My graduate student friends teased me about this and expressed their unanimous opinions that the car would not last beyond my thesis defence. However I had the last laugh, as the car survived several trips between Illinois and Montreal, and finally gave up the ghost in June 1954 when Peggy and I were en route to Quebec City, from which we would embark for Europe for my post-doctoral program.

Martin and Al, along with another Canadian, John Cochran, as well as Meyer Garber from Philadelphia and I made the most of our scholarly situation and formed a *Speisengesellschaft*, or eating club. We ate dinner together most days and then did something afterward, such as watching the planes land at the nearby airport or listening to the corn crack in the fields of Illinois. When a corncob reaches a certain size, its husk is stretched tight and undergoes a discontinuous expansion, which is accompanied by a shot-like noise. We would sit in the car listening to a sequence of discontinuous shots. We would look at each other and nod or shake our heads as though we were connoisseurs and make knowing remarks.

I worked most effectively by going to sleep when tired and waking up when rested. Naturally I found I converted to a twenty-seven-hour cycle. Follow a regime, enjoy your rest: this advice may sound like common sense but it is strange how regimented many individuals' schedules are and yet how few people manage to get proper rest.

When I arrived in Urbana at the beginning of September 1950 and chose Charlie Slichter as my adviser, I discovered that I was part of a very exciting group of researchers. I also discovered that I was more interested in nuclear magnetic resonance (NMR) than in nuclear physics, even though I had originally chosen Urbana in order to work in nuclear physics. NMR was used to probe the structural and dynamical properties of a wide variety of condensed matter systems, which is also true of neutron scattering of a similar range of material. Neither NMR nor neutron scattering turned out to be important at the frontier of nuclear physics, though both made it possible to study fundamental properties of matter. A Nobel prize for NMR was awarded to Edward Purcell (Harvard University) and Felix Bloch (Stanford University) and a Nobel Prize for neutron scattering was shared by Bertram Brockhouse (AECL) and Clifford Shull (Massachusetts Institute of Technology). Ernest Wollan (MIT) was a co-author for this work, but he did not share the prize because he was already dead by the time it was awarded in 1994, and the Nobel Prizes cannot be awarded posthumously.

When I began working with Slichter, he was supervising the PhD theses of Richard Norberg, Don Holcomb and Burton Muller. Norberg was working on the last stages of his dissertation on the NMR spectrum of hydrogen dissolved in solid-state palladium, the first comprehensive study of a solid-state system using NMR. He already had preliminary results under a wide range of temperatures between 2 Kelvin (about −271°C) and room temperature, and at that time he was working at liquid helium temperature, about 4 Kelvin or −269°C. Holcomb built additional equipment and extended these studies still further. When I was ready to do my own research, I was able to use Norberg's equipment to test my own theories and detect the signals that confirmed them. This saved me a lot of time, and Norberg himself was also very helpful. At this time, only one PhD degree had been awarded for NMR research at Urbana, to Erwin Hahn. He stayed on for a few months and discovered the phenomenon of spin-echo signals. This was probably the most important development after the discovery of NMR itself.

Slichter's other graduate student, Burt Muller, had found himself in a blind alley and was working on finding a more fruitful topic. We talked about supercooling in a number of complicated organic molecules, including menthol, being accompanied by a superposition of exponential variations of thermodynamic properties in the transition region. Burt decided to look at the NMR properties to check whether they exhibited this controversial behaviour, and this investigation led to a successful research project. When he was offered a position at the University of Wyoming he felt he could accept it, since he was ready to submit a thesis for his PhD.

In the meantime a lot had happened. Burt got married, and his wife, Jackie, had occasional visits from her former college roommate, Peggy Holmes. I fell in love with Peggy on one of her visits. Peggy's first visit to Urbana took place in 1952. At that time, she was a social worker living in Syracuse, New York. We were both very busy—I had just started on my dissertation research and Peggy's workday far exceeded eight hours, but we did manage to see each other, either in Urbana or in Syracuse. Although we did not have much time together on those visits, I remember the interactions with her co-workers being very lively and enjoyable. My sister Bernice and her husband, Sid, moved to Syracuse around that time and I put them in touch with Peggy. Probably our most important visit was a camping and canoeing trip in Ontario's Algonquin Park. Neither of us had had much experience of this kind, and it put our relationship to the test. Fortunately, we made the best use of campsites, canoe portages and other physically demanding conditions to demonstrate to ourselves that we enjoyed each other's company under unusually challenging circumstances.

Recalling Peggy's visits to campus today reminds me how profoundly customs have changed during the past sixty years. Her first visit occurred about the same time that a post-doctoral fellow, Subrahmanyan Chandrasekhar, arrived from England where he had just completed his PhD at Oxford to take up his two-year position with the low-temperature group in which John Cochran and Meyer Garber were working. There was a welcoming party for Chandra at which we found his reaction to American life to be witty, and so we told him that we would like to introduce him to something unusual, which would require a five-minute walk to a Lincoln Avenue residence hall at midnight. As we entered the residence at 11:59, we heard the nightly announcement reminding students that all male visitors had to leave [by 12:00 a.m]. The rules also required that each couple have three feet on the floor at all times. As the broadcast finished, Chandra exclaimed in his clipped Indo-English accent: "Good heavens, their last moment on earth!"

In my studies, I was exploring all sorts of sub-fields of physics. My supervisor didn't necessarily know about this, though it came up in philosophical discussions about the freedom of graduate students and how they use their time. At that time, the physics department at Illinois was the best in the world to my knowledge. Loomis had decided to make the department outstanding in solid-state physics and had attracted Fred Seitz, who in turn attracted John Bardeen, a Nobel Prize winner for his invention of the transistor. Eventually Bardeen was awarded a second Nobel Prize with Leon Cooper and Bob Schrieffer. Schrieffer was one of Bardeen's graduate students while I was at Urbana. In 1956, I met Cooper at the summer school in Varenna, Italy, while I was doing my post-doc at Leiden. When he found out that I had done my graduate work at Urbana, he approached me to ask about living conditions there, since he had been invited to work with Bardeen. He was (smilingly) certain, sitting in the sunshine on the steps of Villa Monastero at Lago di Como, that he would solve the problem of superconductivity. I have the impression now that he already had the idea that led to "Cooper Pairs," which formed the basis of the BCS (Bardeen-Cooper-Schrieffer) theory of superconductivity.

Also joining the department were outstanding theoretical physicists Geoff Chew and Francis Low, who had left Berkeley in California and MIT in Massachusetts, respectively, because those state governments had established loyalty oaths. During the McCarthy era in the 1950s in the US, professors at some universities in those states were often required to sign an oath affirming their loyalty to the federal constitution and denying that they belonged to or believed in "communist" organizations that were pushing to overthrow the federal government. Chew and Low were working on the physics of pi-mesons, subatomic particles that were considered to be the "glue" that held the nucleus together. Although there was much excitement at the university about their research while I was there, my impression in those days that nuclear physics was going to be the most exciting field has not been borne out. Low- and intermediate-energy nuclear physics have not produced insights leading to understanding since that time.

The arrival of a post-doctoral fellow, Al Overhauser, who was working in the field of electron magnetism in metals, created additional excitement. He predicted that nuclear spin polarization could be enhanced by the microwave irradiation of the conduction electrons in certain metals. He presented his ideas at a meeting attended by some researchers who were working at the forefront of NMR, such as Purcell, Isidor Isaac Rabi, Bloch and Norman Ramsey. None of them believed Overhauser's predictions because they seemed to obviously violate the second law of thermodynamics. However, he suggested some experiments to Charlie Slichter, who asked his graduate student Tom Carver to carry out the experiments. Carver built the necessary apparatus and the experiments verified Overhauser's predictions. Overhauser had shown that it is possible to line up, or polarize, nuclear spins by about 1000 times what common intuitive arguments would predict. By first imposing microwave power on the nuclear-electron system, he was able to excite the electronic spins to higher, non-thermal equilibrium states. Then, because of the coupling between the electron and the nuclear spins, as the excited electron spins tried to equilibrate to their lower states, they reoriented the nuclear spins, resulting in the enhanced polarization. Overhauser's theory was ultimately extended and is now known as the "Nuclear Overhauser Effect."

John Wheatley was an assistant professor in the department, and I saw him nearly every day while I was in Urbana. He had not published anything since his thesis, and my friends from the *Speisengesellschaft* and I expressed our concern about this. He said that he had decided not to publish until he had spent a year acquiring the lore of low-temperature physics. There was no pressure to publish at the University of Illinois, and he had enough confidence to instead develop expertise. When I was at Leiden for my post-doctoral work, he came as a visiting researcher with his own funding. It was apparent that his strategy had been successful, since he was far ahead of the famous group at the Kamerlingh Onnes Laboratory.

After his return to Urbana, he became the best-known low-temperature researcher in the field. W.J. Huiskamp and A.R. Miedema, among the most successful students at the Kamerlingh Onnes lab, modified their own techniques and later joined him as post-docs in Urbana. Eventually Wheatley moved to the University of California at San Diego. One lesson I took from this was that while it is tempting to leave the development of equipment to the technicians, they can get bogged down because they don't have enough theoretical background.

At the time that I was there, Illinois's physics department did not have an expert on relativity. With the support of senior faculty such as Sid Dancoff and Arnold Nordsieck, graduate students and post-docs organized seminars on the subject. I had read a paper by Albert Einstein and Nathan Rosen on the nature of space-time, but I was not getting any help on this personal project in general relativity. However, I figured it out on my own during the period when I was travelling back and forth between Urbana and Montreal. Then George McVittie joined the faculty as a joint appointee of physics and astronomy and started a regular seminar series for which I made a presentation on relativity involving curvature in space-time. For a while I thought I would write a thesis on general relativity, but I also had a lot of ideas about NMR. I used to have conversations with Dave McCall, a fellow graduate student working on NMR in chemistry under Gutowsky. He asked me whether a super-regenerative oscillator would work to detect pure quadrupole resonance (PQR), a system with no large static magnetic field. In PQR, the high-frequency oscillations are associated with differences in energy between orientation of nuclear quadrupole moment and gradient in the crystalline electric field. We did some laboratory investigation and observed free induction and spin-echo signals. Pure quadrupole signals had been observed for steady-state NMR, but we observed magnetic induction signals following a pulse, and spin-echo signals when there was more than one pulse. As a result of these observations, I recognized that in fact the super-regenerative oscillator was detecting PQR and I worked out a proof, which I gave to my supervisor. It was a long presentation involving coupled differential equations, and Slichter tried to avoid going through this mass of papers like any logical person. He gave me a symmetry argument about why it had to be wrong, though he was very generous when it turned out that I was right and he was wrong. This work formed the basis of my PhD thesis: "Free Magnetic Induction in Pure Quadrupole Resonance."

As a result of this work, I was invited to give a paper at the spring meeting of the American Physical Society. I collaborated with two other researchers in this area, Erwin Hahn and Bernard Herzog, to write a comprehensive paper on the theory and experiments of free magnetic induction, which was published as "Free Magnetic Induction in Nuclear Quadrupole Resonance" in *Physical Review* 97. Charlie Slichter told me that it was very impressive and unusual for a graduate student to be included in such a presentation.

It was clear that I was in a field that suited me: NMR was a new field in that whatever was studied was new, there were many puzzles to solve and many "aha" moments to be had. Writing a thesis became easy for me, and, of course, was very pleasurable and paradoxical because I had initially been less interested in NMR since it wasn't nuclear physics.

CHAPTER 5.

POST-DOC IN
POST-WAR LEIDEN

I defended my thesis after I had been married for less than a week. Peggy and I had managed to see each other every few months during those busy years since 1952, and we were married on May 29, 1954. I had already planned to do post-doctoral research and had applied for a National Research Council (NRC) travelling fellowship position at the University of Leiden in the Netherlands, home of the Kamerlingh Onnes (KO) Lab, which was at that time the world leader in the study of low-temperature physics. I was looking forward to taking the spin-echo technique that Erwin Hahn had developed, that I had used in Illinois, and to doing some actual research with it at low temperatures. I was offered one of the first two-year (as opposed to one-year) fellowship positions. Peggy was enthusiastic about the idea of living in Leiden.

In 1954, planes were not yet commercially available and so the best arrangements had to be by ship. Peggy had wanted to organize our travel since I was dealing with the thesis defense, but she had no experience in making these sorts of arrangements and we initially ended up in France instead of Rotterdam. I remember sitting on our trunk, which contained all our belongings and smelled to high heaven because we had a bottle of whiskey in there that had broken, until we caught another boat to Rotterdam. Travelling by boat seems now such a different way of travelling.

Travelling was very important to me. My first experiences had been the small trips my basketball team took when I was an athlete, and these were also very important to me. However, Thomas Wolfe was one of my favourite authors and he also influenced my thoughts on travel. I had read every book this guy had written. He had been brought up around North Carolina and was one of the first notable writers trained in creative writing at university. His four novels, which took place in pre-war America, were split into two parts. The first half was always about leaving home and the second was about returning. There was said to be a famous relationship between him and his editor, Maxwell Perkins, in that the books were a real triumph of editing and Wolfe never would have published on his own. The key points about travelling that I had captured from Wolfe's books were the excitement of looking into other people's faces (fiercely) and the beginning motion on a train and how it related to the sounds in your mind.

Peggy and I had nothing arranged when we arrived in Holland. Since we had arrived before the lab opened, we had time to make a trip to Italy with a couple we had met on the boat who had rented a car. They were visiting all the cathedrals and major art galleries in Milan, Florence,

Venice and Rome, and it was an educational experience for me. In fact, we were so impressed with Michelangelo's statue of *David* in Florence that we named our first child David.

However, when we returned to Leiden, we needed to find a place to live. Peggy had written a letter to the housing office, and it became a hilarious affair. She had tried to make the inquiry amusing, and we discovered that the housing office had not understood that we were actually looking for living quarters. But in the end it all worked out very well.

Holland was recovering from the war. As a nation they're very good planners, always prepared to make sacrifices for the good of the nation. Salaries were controlled at this point, and professors, presidents and fellows at the university all took home the same amount of money. The salary provided by my grant was comparable, and we were able to rent a decent place from a formidable-looking Dutch woman. She was a widow, and she claimed that her husband, who played viola, had joined Einstein, an average violinist, in chamber music. There was lots of music in the city, especially lots of string orchestras playing music in churches in the morning...

In the room we rented, there was a bed, a large window that opened onto the garden, two burners, a small icebox and a shared toilet on the second floor. It was very interesting to cook because you could only get what was in season. For example, in winter it was cabbage and cauliflower; fish was always in good supply, lots of uncooked, lightly salted *groene haring*. We often went to the nearby Café Sport, where we had a social life. The clients were middle-class residents of the suburb that began at the tram stop located at our front door. We frequently travelled by tram to the seaside villages Katwijk and Noordwijk, where I was amused by the observation that all the villagers looked alike. The teenage boys and girls played the "bumping game" as they walked along the boardwalk. This seemed to me to be a fisherman's version of the kind of behaviour in which I had participated as a teenager in Montreal, when my friends and I went walking on Park Avenue after the Passover seders or the Baron Byng High School concerts.

We were plunged into this Dutch culture, and it was just great. We could go all over the country by bike and train, though I was never a good bike rider so every trip was an adventure. While exploring the canals, I noticed a sign at the entrance to a well-known café (De Doelen) saying that the Leiden Chess Club, Leidsch Schaakgenootschap, met there every Wednesday evening. The next Wednesday I entered the café and found about forty chess games in progress. I received a warm welcome from the chairman who suggested that I play a match and, if I was interested, they would be glad to have me as a member. When he found that my name was "Bloem," he introduced me to seventy-five-year-old Mijnheer Bloem who defeated me in about twenty moves. After I played a second game with a similar result, I joined the club and became eligible to join a team of ten that was entered in regular monthly matches against other teams of the same calibre. The best player in the club was Max Euwe, who was World Chess Champion between 1937 and 1939, and played Board One of the first team. Everyone was eligible to play in a national league no matter what their ability. In my league, I played Board Five at the tenth level. After I'd been in Holland for almost a year, I was approached by the organizer of a basketball team composed of Canadian residents in Holland. My ranking in the basketball league was much higher than my ranking in the chess league!

The Dutch language lends itself to humour. For example, the Dutch word for "canal" is *gracht* and the "g" and "ch" are both pronounced like someone clearing their throat. The first sentence I learned from my Dutch language book was *"Chrietje, gooi geen groene in de gele gracht"* (which means "Gretchen, don't throw green vegetables into the yellow canal"), where each "ch" and "g" sounds like throat-clearing. I had a big advantage over Peggy, since I knew both Yiddish and French, which helped with pronunciation and some free vocabulary. Dutch and Yiddish are both German-based languages with some similar words.

My research in the KO lab had two components during my first year in Leiden. I spent the first few weeks trying to be helpful in the experiment being carried on in the measurement of the crystalline water protons in the compound copper chloride dihydrate. Compounds of this sort had been studied at the KO lab by Nicolaas Bloembergen in his PhD thesis. The first work I completed was a theoretical analysis of spin lattice relaxation in low-temperature anti-ferromagnetic materials, which was used to interpret NMR data obtained in the KO lab by the group of Dr. N.J. Poulis. I was learning how the lab worked, but I did not yet have the equipment to conduct my own research. Gorter said he was confident that the director of Philips Research Lab, Hendrik Casimir, who was an honorary professor at Leiden, would be glad to request that a broadband Intermediate Frequency receiver strip be constructed to my specifications by the end of the year.

I completed an experimental project during my first year in Leiden, for which I constructed and tested a pulsed NMR spectrometer. The technicians were wonderful guys who had set up an instrument school and had developed a device that allowed us to liquefy helium. The world was changing: you didn't have to be able to liquefy your own helium in one of a few places in the world. You could buy a helium liquefier. Luckily, I was able to renew my NRC travelling fellowship at the end of the first year, since otherwise I would not have had the time to make measurements with the new spectrometer.

There were shocking differences between the American and Dutch ways of doing science. I felt the Americans were way ahead in their approach to physics. In my first year in Leiden, a doctoral student told me they had some really interesting results but they had no clue how to explain them. I stayed over Easter break in a closed lab; to do this, I needed special permission in order to get in and then had to feel my way to the light switches. I was elated because I felt I was on the brink of something. It was a big lab, and there were many research groups. My work was connected with one of the groups supervised by Dr. Poulis, and I had been given a plot of the data that the team had recently acquired. The new results just supplemented the previous data. I saw that for this range of temperatures, there was a much bigger change than anticipated in the thermodynamic properties of copper sulphate, accompanied by a change in the magnetization of the NMR lines.

At the time of these experiments, the accepted picture was the one that had been developed for ferromagnetic materials. However, the material under investigation in the Poulis lab was anti-ferromagnetic, and I used the data to develop a model for magnetization as a function of relaxation time, which showed that the relaxation time increased more rapidly than had previously been appreciated as the magnetization approached saturation value. We saw that there was an anisotropy to the magnetic field produced by the domains of magnetism, and part of the story characterizing the collective motions of the electrons involves the generation of waves that spread the effect over many atoms.

Professor Gorter was the first to return to the lab after the break, and when he found me alone there he asked me what I was doing. I told him that I was waiting for Dr. Poulis to get back, so I could discuss the ideas I had about what I had just learned. Gorter wanted to know more, and when I told him what I had done, he thought that I should talk with Jan van Kranendonk, a theoretical physicist who had been hired by the Lorentz Institute and had just arrived from Amsterdam. Van Kranendonk was working on spin waves, and Gorter said it sounded to him as though my model was equivalent to spin wave theory. By the time Poulis returned, I had already contacted van Kranendonk and he had agreed to supervise me in setting up a quantitative theory of spin waves in anti-ferromagnetic materials. Poulis was upset because he had once had his data stolen by a post-doctoral fellow, who had published his results without any acknowledgement of Poulis's contribution. Poulis assumed that I was trying to repeat this kind of unethical use of his results, and he told his students not to discuss their work with me. Part of my shock at his lack of trust was because we had previously enjoyed social contact. Peggy and I had visited his home in Katwijk aan Zee and Poulis's wife had returned the visit.

I was of the attitude that theoreticians and experimentalists should talk to each other as much as possible, but this was not the Dutch practice. It was very strange for me to work in a place where my fellow scientists weren't talking to me. But I had my part of the lab, I could still do low-temperature experiments and I continued to work with van Kranendonk. We wrote a paper together on the theory of relaxation in anti-ferromagnetic materials, and my work on nuclear relaxation theory was published in collaboration with van Kranendonk and was one of several papers recognized as contributing to spin wave relaxation theory of ordered magnetic systems. Poulis himself published an alternative theory using a different approach.

In the last part of my stay in Leiden, I wrote three papers on my measurements of the relaxation times in molecular hydrogen. Shortly afterward, these papers were cited by Anatole Abragam in his book on nuclear magnetism. Poulis suggested that one of his graduate students could continue my work after I left Leiden, and he asked me to explain to this student how the apparatus worked. When I saw Poulis many years later at a meeting we both attended, he was very cordial.

One of the attractions of studying in Europe was that I could expect to attend lectures given by some of the people who were famous for their contributions to the advancement of physics in the first half of the twentieth century. The war had ended by the time I began my studies in 1945, and many of the famous scientists who had contributed to quantum mechanics and relativity were still living when I arrived in Leiden. I could expect to meet some of them and hear their stories.

Wolfgang Pauli was a famous theoretical physicist of the twentieth century who is given credit for proposing the existence of the neutrino in the early 1930s. He postulated two particles, the neutron and the neutrino, in order to avoid having to discard conservation of energy, momentum and angular momentum. He came to Leiden while I was there, and he gave a lecture on the evening of the Ehrenfest Colloquium. Whenever he made such a visit, all the physics professors in Holland were invited to a special lecture on the afternoon of that day. All others were excluded. My friend Meyer Garber and I decided to attend the lecture, and we told the person guarding the door that we insisted on being allowed to attend Pauli's lecture. We promised to be quiet and well behaved if we were allowed to attend. The chairman of the session was Uhlenbech, who had been appointed as the first Lorentz Professor for one year. Uhlenbech announced the title of the session: "Why the Shafroth Theory of Superconductivity is Wrong," and said that to make sure everyone knew the background, Casimir, the leading solid-state physicist of the time, would state the problem. He did that and gave a very nice lecture, and several times during this lecture, Pauli said: "Shafroth is wrong." Uhlenbech would interject with comments like, "Casimir is just giving the background; you'll have your chance." Several questions were asked of Casimir, who answered them. When Pauli gave his lecture and was asked a question, he responded by giving a reference to a paper that had recently been published in *Physica* and told the questioner that he could find the answer there. I thought Uhlenbech had asked Casimir to give the introduction because he knew that Pauli would not recognize the need for some background. In fact, it took several years for theoretical developments to progress far enough to correct the flaws Pauli had found in Shafroth's theory.

When I describe my experimental program as it evolved at UBC in my own independent laboratory, it will be apparent that the three papers I wrote in Leiden on molecular hydrogen in the gas, liquid and solid phases allowed me to develop a very fruitful line of research. I was confident I would succeed in generating a high standard in my research program because good research mainly requires proposing unusual questions that advance our knowledge and insight about nature. In 1954, NMR was equivalent to having a new language with which to communicate with nature, and the discovery of pulsed NMR by Erwin Hahn was equivalent to having found a previously unknown dialect. Almost all material had nuclear spins and therefore gave rise to NMR signals.

Peggy had gone back to New York City after the first

year in Leiden. She had the problem most Americans had, which was language difficulties. It looked as though our marriage was breaking up. Peggy was a social worker, but when we married and moved to Leiden, she had had to give up social work. She had tried other things, like being an artist, and she painted some memorable scenes, including Molen de Velk, the famous windmill by Leiden's Centraal Station. She had also joined a choral society at the University of Leiden, but although she enjoyed being in Holland, she was left out in a number of ways and life there was difficult for her. When she decided to leave, it was with the understanding she would separate from me; however, after being in New York for half a year, she decided to come back to me upon my return from Leiden.

So in my second year in Holland I was on my own, and at first I thought it was permanent. This meant that I was going on dates and such, or a Dutch version of a date. You'd meet a woman in a café, then you would have to give her a ride on the back of your bike after you met. I was very interesting to locals; Canadians were highly thought of because our soldiers had liberated Holland. I always had drinks bought for me, usually beer or *genever* (Dutch gin), and got immediately into local conversation.

Early in 1955, a notice appeared on the board at the KO lab for a summer school program on nuclear physics, organized by Enrico Fermi and the Italian Physical Society. It was to take place in the small mountain town of Varenna, on Lago di Como in northern Italy. This was the third such summer school, and the first two had set a high standard. The speakers were outstanding. Peggy was preparing to leave in early June, and I was hoping to begin my experiment when the lab reopened in September. Attending this program seemed like an ideal way of combining a summer school with some travel. I applied and got in, and even received a fellowship to support my stay. I think everything I ever really tried to get, I got.

Pauli always came to the summer schools, and he was at Varenna when I went to my first summer school there. He liked being a presence, and he attended all the talks given by both students and faculty. Pauli really concentrated when attending these talks, and students developed a habit of closely monitoring his reactions while the talks were being given. When a novel point was made by the speaker, Pauli would nod his head either up and down or side to side, depending on whether he agreed or disagreed, and modifying his initial response, if necessary. The students were amused and respected his opinions, so that Pauli acted as a kind of pope for the talks.

In my second year, I became friendly with Irwin Oppenheim, an American who had a sports car and lived two blocks down from me. Once we got to know each other, he came over often. About every second night we went out in his car. Irwin was a gourmet; he had lunch every weekday with the theoretical physics group at a restaurant close to the Lorentz Institute, and I often joined them for an hour of stimulating conversation with Sybren de Groot and his girlfriend, Sylvia. In 1955 Sybren and Peter Mazur founded the Lorentz Institute of Theoretical Physics in Leiden.

During the Christmas break, I went to Britain and looked up Trudi Goldschmidt, who was now married and had two young children. She was visiting her mother,

Laura, and I was able to stay in her mother's home. Laura Goldschmidt had just bought a car but couldn't drive because she had been in two consecutive accidents. She said she would enjoy a drive to Italy to tour the opera houses. Since my good friend John Cochran was planning to visit over spring break, I suggested that if John would share the driving, we could do this trip together.

After the Christmas break, I felt I had to begin looking for a permanent job. I had enjoyed being in Europe where everything was a new experience and people were more at my level in terms of professional knowledge. I felt I was interacting with people like Purcell who had discovered NMR. At the same time, I had a lot of interest in returning to Canada, so I wrote to some people there. I had no desire to go back to the States. My correspondence at UBC was with George M. Volkoff, a well-known theoretical physicist who had set up an experimental NMR group. They had developed a method of analyzing resonance for systems having quadrupolar interactions, and I felt that my work and interests would fit in very well. Volkoff also felt that UBC would have a position of interest to me. However, I didn't hear from Volkoff for two months, even though I wrote a letter requesting details of the UBC faculty position for which I might apply.

In the meantime, I had been offered a position at Gif-sur-Yvette in France, with the new Commissariat à l'énergie atomique, that interested me. The leader of this group in Paris was Anatole Abragam who had just written a definitive book on NMR. This was January 1956, and I had not yet heard from Volkoff about the UBC position. I wrote to Abragam that I found his job to be attractive, and after an exchange of letters, I agreed to a deadline of just after Easter for my response, in part because of the plans Laura Goldschmidt, John Cochran and I were making to drive to Rome. Finally, Volkoff came through with a definite commitment just before I left on the trip to Italy.

Our trip to Italy was a frivolous one. We planned to visit the great opera houses of Italy and to listen to at least one opera per day for one week and to partake of several aspects of Italian culture, such as food and wine and art. I felt that it would be best to make an important decision (such as which of two excellent possibilities I should choose for my first salaried job with prospects of long-term stability) while I was relaxed. By contrast, it would probably be unwise for me to make such a decision while preoccupied with details of a research problem. I'm not sure that the same criteria would apply to most people but that's the way I felt.

On our return from Italy we stopped in Paris, where Laura left us to go home to England. John and I continued to Leiden, and I introduced him to a secretary of the physics department, Pieternella. He threw the keys of the car across the room to me and told me to take a drive, which I did. At that time John was doing post-doctoral work with Kurt Mendelssohn in low-temperature physics at Oxford University in England, but he also had a travelling fellowship and was able to continue his work at the KO lab in Leiden. He and Pieternella got married soon afterward, and I consider introducing them one of the really great things I've done because they've had a wonderful marriage.

Several days before we'd reached Paris, I'd known I had

left My high school graduation photo, from 1945. I attended Baron Byng High School in Montreal, as did literary greats Mordecai Richler and Irving Layton.

below In high school I became serious about athletics, a passion that would continue throughout my life. I went on to play basketball for McGill University.

right In formal wear with my Uncle Louis (on the right), at the wedding of one of my cousins, around 1948.

below Montreal's YMHA (now the Jewish Community Centre) had a group called the "Cosmos Club" that I participated in. We held regular philosophical discussions and social activities. I am the third one from the left in the back row.

top Peggy Holmes was a social worker when we met. We got married on May 29, 1954, and this photo from that day shows her sense of humour.

bottom I bought this Oldsmobile for about $100 from a fellow graduate student in a nuclear physics course at the University of Illinois. It was the first car built with an automatic transmission and made a lot of noise.

top From the left: Martha Piper, former president and vice-chancellor of the University of British Columbia; me; and my wife, Peggy. This photo was taken before I received an honorary Doctor of Science degree from UBC on May 25, 2000.

bottom From the left: UBC professor Michael Smith (a Nobel Prize winner for chemistry in 1993), me and UBC professor emeritus David Williams.

top My two children, Margot and David. Margot has used her expertise in movement therapy to help me with coordination and muscle tone in dealing with the effects of Parkinson's disease. David writes, produces and directs theatre projects in Vancouver.

bottom My sister Bernice and me. She was instrumental in helping me complete the writing of this book.

top I first met Walter Hardy when he was one of my graduate students at UBC. He became a life-long friend. He is now professor emeritus in UBC's Department of Physics and Astronomy.

bottom An outstanding scientist and now professor emeritus in UBC's Department of Physics and Astronomy, Evan Evans was a long-time collaborator of mine.

above On September 13, 2007, a symposium was held at UBC, in my honour. Here I am surrounded by many of my closest friends, family members and collaborators.

left Danish scientist Ole Mouritsen did a travelling fellowship at UBC with me in the late 1970s. We built a lasting friendship during those two years.

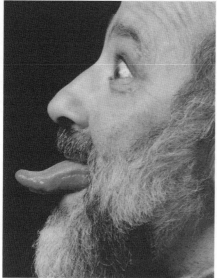

above Members of the Canadian Institute for Advanced Research's Soft Surfaces and Interfaces Program, a multidisciplinary, international team of scientists established in 1982. From left to right: David Boal, Adrian Parsegian, Terrance Beveridge, Sidney Simon, me, Erich Sackmann, Evan Evans, Mohandas Narla and Jacques Prost.

left I forget now what point I was making in this lecture at UBC, but this is my demonstration of a stimulated response.

to accept the UBC offer even though most of the logical arguments I considered could easily have persuaded me to accept the Paris offer. On our stopover, Abragam had invited me to his home and his wife, Suzanne, prepared an impressive French meal. He spent the evening trying to persuade me to change my mind and join his exciting group, but my mind was made up. Even though Abragam was able to offer me about twice the salary that I'd earn at UBC, when it came right down to it, I really wanted to be independent. I'd just spent four years of PhD study and two years as a post-doc working with brilliant people. Abragam was a really forceful and insightful researcher, and I would have had difficulty working fast enough to keep ahead of him. In retrospect, I realize I knew it would be a good idea to escape from all these clever people and give myself room for my own ideas.

I might well have enjoyed working with Abragam's group, which established itself very quickly. I would also have enjoyed living in France on a long-term basis, but I was not sure if my marriage would have survived several years in France. During the year we were separated, Peggy and I had been communicating. We both realized that we wanted to resume our relationship, and when I informed her that I would have to choose between jobs in Vancouver or in Paris, she indicated she would be okay with either decision. However, I was not sure that she would be able to learn French. She was an American citizen and had not been exposed to any foreign languages before we went to the Netherlands together.

Before I left Europe, I went back to Varenna to attend the summer school. This time the focus was on my field, magnetism (including magnetic resonance), and the best people were there. These included Charles Kittel and Walter Knight from Berkeley, Mendelssohn, Nicholas Kurti and Brebis Bleaney from the Clarendon Lab at Oxford, Abragam from Paris, Purcell from Harvard, Gorter from the KO lab at Leiden and Ryogo Kubo from Japan. On one of the days, Kubo was giving two lectures separated by the lunch break. In the first session he was showing how important Linear Response Theory was as the basis of nuclear spin relaxation theory, but the audience clearly was not able to follow the argument. During the break I was walking with Kubo, and I told him that I had not understood and that I knew Purcell and Abragam also had not been able to follow the argument. He thanked me and tried to clarify the argument in the second lecture. He made it clear that he had appreciated my comments and that he considered me a friend.

Pauli was also attending this summer school, and he took my friend and collaborator Jan van Kranendonk for a walk along the Lago di Como. Van Kranendonk had written a paper on a theory for spin waves, which is a theoretical model for understanding magnetism. On average these waves are pointing in some direction, and you can understand the magnetic properties in terms of all the waves being lined up in the same direction. He modelled them as being in a kind of gas, with these spins propagating through the system. On the walk, Pauli said to him: "The first page of your three papers was very interesting. Why didn't you keep it up?" Van Kranendonk had already written a lot at a very young age, and Pauli was saying that the first page was good but the rest of it was garbage. It was typical Pauli. Known for being critical, he once said of a particular piece of work: "This is not worth publishing; it isn't even wrong."

CHAPTER 6.

UBC AND THE RESEARCH HIGH

I returned to North America on a regular steamboat that carried cargo from Rotterdam to New York. It was a great experience, as there were only ten passengers and we were served meals with the captain and the other officers. And when he heard I was a physicist, the second mate asked me for help because he was preparing for his first-mate exam and was having some trouble with calculus.

When I reached New York City, Peggy was there to meet me. We then travelled by train from New York City to Seattle by way of Montreal. (Travel by airplane was uncommon in 1956, and travel by commercial airlines using jet planes was essentially non-existent.) The changes in scenery as we crossed the continent were dramatic. Before planning our travel, I had learned there would be an international conference on theoretical physics in Seattle at about the time we would reach that city en route to Vancouver. It was easy to time our travelling and tourism to allow me to attend the conference. By then I knew and was friends with many theoretical physicists. One of them was Gordon Feldman, who had been a summer student at Chalk River during the same period as me. He had been a post-doctoral fellow in Birmingham, England, with the famous theoretical physicist R.E. Peierls, and at the Institute for Advanced Study at Princeton University while I was a post-doc in Leiden. When Gordon met me in Seattle he said that it was going to be an exciting conference, and indeed it was. C.N. Yang (Princeton) and T.D. Lee (Columbia) had succeeded in producing a new theory that resolved controversies about recent discoveries in nuclear physics. I felt that Yang and Lee had shifted the frontiers of physical science outward and a few months later even the *New York Times* described the excitement created in Seattle when it ran a feature article about this theory in its January 10, 1957, edition. New experiments followed shortly afterward.

The last stage of the trip was by ferry boat from Seattle to Vancouver. We were full of anticipation for the mountains and sea characteristic of Vancouver. As we entered Vancouver harbour, however, it became evident that Nature was not going to allow us to see her magnificent features easily. We could see water for only a short distance ahead because of thick fog and the summits were only visible to about 6000 feet because of clouds. Volkoff met us at the ferry and told us that this type of fog and cloud were common in the fall and that we would eventually see the beautiful mountains. It took a month before we could see the mountains from the city or the city from the mountains, and this provided Peggy with a humorous theme for her first month's artwork.

A positive aspect of our move to UBC was that suitable housing had been arranged in advance. During the war,

UBC had developed a training program for technologists and others working in fields related to the war effort. Inexpensive houses had been constructed for the increased number of students, but after the war ended these were made available for faculty as well as students and staff. As he showed us to our new home, Volkoff expressed his regret at the low salaries but hoped they would improve soon, allowing us to compete for market housing. This did happen, and all of my colleagues with families were able to buy houses close to UBC. No one predicted how much those land values would increase, though it was generally believed that a substantial increase was likely, and a typical house that cost about $20,000 in 1956 sold for about $1.5 million in 2014.

At the time, my wife and I were considered eccentric because we loved the student-faculty community in Acadia Camp and had no desire to buy a house. Our son, David, was born there in 1959 and our daughter, Margot, in 1962. Meanwhile, I was promoted to associate professor in 1960 and to full professor in 1963. My application for a sabbatical leave in 1964–65 at Harvard and Kyoto had already been approved, and I had arranged for someone to occupy our UBC apartment in our absence. However, upon my return to UBC in 1965, the new housing director informed me that we were no longer eligible for faculty housing because I was earning too much money as a full professor. He said: "You have lots of time to buy a house," and, that very day, Peggy rented a house two blocks from Acadia Camp. The three-storeyed townhouses on Kings Road each had four units. There were no boundaries between the four-unit houses so the play area behind the houses was common to all the children on Kings Road. Peggy had written a master's thesis in social work on community planning and she could see many good features in the Kings Road design with regard to communication between children and adults in a small community. She explained to me how similar the Kings Road community was to the St. Dominique Street community of my childhood, even though the design of the houses was quite different.

Our social life was enlivened by the fact that our next-door neighbour, Ian Smart, was a member of the Scottish Dancing Society, which met one evening a week at various members' homes. The dancing was followed by consuming beer brewed by that member. Peggy and I joined the group after Ian made an impassioned speech in his deep Scottish accent about how pleasurable it was after a hard day's work to see millions of bacteria working for you and how home-brewed beer satisfied the enhanced thirst brought on by the dancing!

At the time I arrived at UBC, the university was losing some of its best people to other institutions that offered higher salaries and lower teaching loads, and one of the reasons was that Vancouver had a higher cost of housing than many other places. In 1958, the head of the faculty association, Jim Foulks, came to see me, along with Bill Gibson, who was chairman of the association's housing committee. They felt that the need for housing for new faculty was desperate and asked me to work with them on a proposal for a new kind of housing. On a visit to attend a Physical Society meeting at Stanford University in California, I discussed this problem with Harden McConnell, a very well-known chemist. He invited me to his home, and I discovered that Stanford had solved this problem by building non-market housing for which only new faculty were eligible. Residents could stay as long as they wished, but the resale prices were controlled by a set of rules. McConnell told me that the housing was not luxurious but highly satisfactory, and he also said that his next-door neighbour was Linus Pauling.

Ultimately, we suggested to the university president, Larry MacKenzie, that he could propose a strategy to the board of governors to get around the financial and sewage-treatment issues that were preventing the construction of more housing near the university. The board of governors rejected our proposal. The dean of commerce, Earle MacPhee, explained that the president could not support a substantial increase in on-campus housing because it was so hard to project student enrollment. I reported this fact at a general meeting of the faculty association, and we kept on trying to influence the provincial government, the Social Credit Party at the time, but the only opinion that mattered was that of the premier, and W.A.C. Bennett said no. Eventually the city constructed the Highbury Tunnel to transport sewage from the northern shores of Point Grey to Iona Island, where there is an industrial area, and this made it possible to build more housing.

During our correspondence, Volkoff had offered me a choice of two positions: an assistant professorship, which is the usual starting position in the academic system and assumes that time will be equally divided between teaching and research, and a research associateship. The salaries for the two positions were almost identical and so I chose the research position because I believed, correctly as it turned out, that the teaching position would reduce the intensity of my research effort at a time that demanded all my energy. None of us knew that we were about to enter an era of increased opportunity for research in the physical sciences in American and Canadian universities. I was looking forward to teaching, but felt it better to make the transition to teaching and research in two steps. As it happened, my salary came from Volkoff's research grant and I acquired teaching experience in an agreeable manner by being a guest lecturer for Volkoff when he travelled as a member of national and international committees concerned with science.

I had known of Volkoff's work before I came to UBC, but several newly appointed faculty, of whom I knew nothing, were also very interesting to me. They had been appointed by Gordon M. Shrum, the head of the department. Each year, Shrum placed an ad in *Nature* and in the *London Times,* and then spent a week in London recruiting. He had confidence in his judgment of potential faculty and he deserves credit for attracting strong people to the physics department.

Shrum was a charismatic and energetic department chair, but his dictatorial leadership style led to special problems. For example, at department meetings, which took place every Monday at noon, Shrum promoted conflict because often he went his own way in spite of general agreement among the faculty in favour of a different course of action. At more general meetings, he never wanted a member of the department to express a different view from what he was proposing.

Another problem involved the graduate courses, which were all one-unit courses with one lecture per week. At one point, a research faction within the department fostered a rebellion while Shrum was away on an extended trip. That group presented a petition for three-unit courses to give more depth to the specialist courses, such as solid-state physics, nuclear physics and non-equilibrium thermodynamics. When Shrum returned, I presented the petition and he acknowledged that I was in charge of course content and could have done a better job. He promised to improve his performance as chairman but refused to give up any authority regarding decisions about the graduate courses. His main argument was that he wanted students to meet with a wide variety of faculty members in the classroom. Several months later, the research faction met and agreed that nothing had changed. Shrum was nearly sixty-five, which meant his retirement was imminent, and we decided to wait until then to make changes to the organization of the graduate courses.

Shrum's range of authority included many administrative positions: Head of Physics, Dean of Graduate Studies, Director of the BC Research Council, Director of Housing. Shrum took his duties seriously. As the head of the housing department, he had many opportunities to use his personal judgment. On one occasion, he told me to remove my wife's bicycle from the laundry room. On another occasion, after attending a beer party that I had thrown at my house for the engineering physics class,

Shrum sent a memo in which he said that he had appreciated my party but added: "Please see me." When I got to his office, he said: "When I was in your house, I noticed you have more than one cat. As you know, you signed a lease saying you would not have cats at all. Up to now I have overlooked this, but one of your cats has shit in a child's sandbox, and the father of this child is president of the student council." He put on his hat and said: "Speaking as head of the department, I cannot help with your dispute with the head of housing. The physiology department will pay ten dollars for a cat and treats them kindly." We did take two cats to physiology, but we kept our favourite one.

When Shrum retired from UBC, he was appointed Chair of BC Electric Company (later BC Hydro), a private company that had a monopoly on controlling electricity in the province. He was also appointed Chancellor of Simon Fraser University (SFU), which was then in the planning stages, and his responsibilities included setting up a highly successful architectural competition for construction of the new campus. Arthur Erickson's firm won the competition, and this project made Erickson's reputation as an architect.

Shortly after Shrum's retirement, George Volkoff told me confidentially that he would become head of the physics department very soon. He also told me that if the National Research Council grant selection committee agreed, he would recommend that his research grant, one of the largest of the smaller grants, be transferred to me. This meant that I would receive a larger starting grant than was normal, which would have a beneficial effect on my research. In effect, I was treated as a senior researcher moving from one place to another. In a very conservative granting system, this was equivalent to several years' advantage.

The Department of Physics at UBC turned out to be very suitable for me. I had acquired a taste for doing experimental physics in an environment in which there were good physicists who enjoyed talking about general principles, and I found such people in the physics department at UBC. Volkoff had obtained his PhD with J. Robert Oppenheimer and had written an important paper on neutron stars. He had worked on nuclear reactors during the war along with Phil Wallace, both in Montreal and at Chalk River. After the war, Volkoff had returned to his alma mater, UBC, and initiated experimental NMR studies along with several PhD students. At that time the university had not yet awarded a PhD in any field, and the first PhD was given to Tom Collins, Volkoff's student, in 1950. Volkoff developed a theoretical method for analyzing spectra of crystals that had significant Zeeman bipolar and quadrupolar interactions, the "Volkoff Method."

Volkoff's lab contained two magnets, a permanent magnet and an electromagnet whose field could be varied by controlling the current and was being used by a PhD student, Lloyd Robinson, who was hoping to satisfy the requirements for his doctorate within a year. Robinson and Volkoff were stuck at the moment. They were applying Volkoff's method to analyze certain transition probabilities, but this method only took into account the x-component of angular momentum. They were using a cross-coil spectrometer for which the x-component of angular momentum in the rotating frame was associated with one coil and the y-component was associated with the other coil, but this had not yet been introduced into the theory. I had experienced this kind of issue in my PhD thesis research, and I had solved the problem within a few weeks at that time. I suggested that they needed to take both dimensions into account, and this solved their problem. We ended up writing a paper together entitled "On the Theory of Nuclear Quadrupole Resonance." As an aside, I can now advise young PhDs that when they start their new jobs in research labs, they bring a fresh point of view and may be well positioned to make new progress on a problem that has been found frustrating.

In addition to Volkoff, the most notable theoreticians in the department were Fred Kaempffer, Wladyslaw Opechowski and Robert Barrie. Kaempffer was interested in the fundamental questions of quantum mechanics and general relativity. He gave a popular colloquium each year on his current interest that always provoked controversy. He also taught a course for the nursing students for a number of years that was well received. Kaempffer once remarked that for the nurses, he used the same notes that he used for his graduate quantum mechanics course, but with a different emphasis. Opechowski was primarily interested in statistical mechanics and his work was characterized by excellent logic. I found that any discussion with him brought a lot of new ideas. Barrie, whose research area was theoretical solid-state physics, joined the department around the same time as I did and we shared an office for many years. He was a rigorous thinker and conversations with him opened up an array of new ideas. Ron Burgess was head of the solid-state group and an expert on stochastic processes. He was an authority and I found that I learned a lot when speaking with him because stochastic processes are very important in NMR.

Volkoff, Kaempffer, Opechowski and Burgess had all been on the faculty for several years when I arrived. The department was growing very rapidly, since once the *Sputnik* satellite had been launched, the number and quality of students interested in physics increased. Jim and Betty Daniels, along with Jim Brown, composed the low-temperature group and had joined the department more recently. In fact, I had met the Danielses at a meeting in Paris in 1955 when I was considering the position at UBC, because they were already in the department and Volkoff had suggested that I talk with them. They were the ones who told Peggy and me about the Scottish Dancing Society.

From the time of my arrival, I worked closely with the low-temperature group and, in particular, with Jim Daniels. We both felt comfortable reading each other's scientific research papers. In 1957 I was at a meeting of the American Physical Society in California, where I encountered George Pake, who had just moved to Stanford from Washington University in St. Louis. Pake told me that Stanford University was looking for an assistant professor whose research interest was in low-temperature physics. He asked whether I knew of any possible candidates, and I told him that Bill Little, a post-doc with a travelling fellowship, was sharing my lab and that he would be a superb candidate. He was nominally working with Jim Daniels, but Jim was preoccupied with his own problems and Bill had been working completely on his own, doing research at extremely low temperatures. Bill was invited to apply for the Stanford position and got the job. He rose quickly and became well known for his work in organic superconductors.

Ironically, Jim Daniels left UBC rather suddenly in the middle of a term to go to Argentina, leaving others in the department to take care of his graduate students and his classes. Fortunately I was able to assist Klaus Rieckhoff, who had almost completed his doctoral research, in finding an external examiner acceptable to the Faculty of Graduate Studies, and I also found someone for David Griffiths. They were outstanding students: Rieckhoff found a job immediately after graduation and came back to Vancouver to become one of the first faculty members in physics at SFU when it opened. Griffiths was working on his own, and he completed his thesis on a project Jim had suggested on the optical detection of magnetic polarization about a year later, and then obtained a position at Oregon State University. Before David Griffiths's departure, another graduate student, Hans Glättli, was accepted by the department and decided to continue Griffiths's work under my supervision. In practice, he received all the guidance he needed from Griffiths and produced an outstanding thesis. Hans completed his thesis in less than three years and then obtained a permanent job with Anatole Abragam in France. Jim eventually returned to Canada when he was offered a position at the University of Toronto. However, I was annoyed at his sudden depar ture because he had left me and other colleagues to complete his faculty responsibilities without notice. He had also left behind his wife, Betty, although he had taken their children with him.

Jim Brown also left UBC a couple of years later, but the low-temperature group continued to be a strong presence in the department, with contributions from other newly arriving faculty such as Dave Williams, Peter Matthews, Mike Crooks, Brian Turrell and Andrew Gold.

Peter Rastall, whose research interests lay in relativity theory, was appointed about the same time as I was and he was my best friend among the physics faculty for my first twenty years. He had a quirky approach to life and I thought of him as being an angry young man, which was a literary allusion of that era. His style was very lively, in physics and in life. His first theoretical seminar included a story about a conflict between two societies, "Ane" and "Teligent." He said that the three senior theoretical faculty (Volkoff, Opechowski and Kaempffer) were "in Ane." A young physicist named Rastall led the three home "in Teligent." This story aroused quite a storm, but he got tenure anyway. I found Peter's research interesting, but our friendship was mostly based on hiking in the local mountains. We also enjoyed the lively late-night jazz performances at the Cellar, a club at the trisection of Main, Kingsway and Broadway, and the folk music at the Question Mark on Broadway. Peter enjoyed poetry, and the people we sat with made contributions that Peter would turn into a poem that he would read aloud. We became local characters at that club, which was frequently visited by Ed McCurdy and other well-known folk singers.

One year, Peter and I introduced a motion at the annual general meeting of the Faculty Club that there be no dress regulations, after the manager had imposed a rule that jackets and ties were to be worn in the dining room and bar. Peter gave an angry young man's speech in making his motion, and I wore a cut-up jacket to illustrate that rules cannot dictate good taste in dress. There was tremendous attendance at the meeting, and the only dissenting vote was by Malcolm McGregor (Classics). As a result of the faculty's reaction to our motion, I was elected to the board of directors of the Faculty Club.

I shared my own lab with David Williams, who arrived in our department in 1960 having just obtained his PhD from Cambridge, where he had studied the properties of metals and superconductivity. He thought he could get the most experience by measuring relaxation time in gases and also check his results using the overlap between his measurements and those made by Max Lipsicas, another researcher in my lab. He decided to work on a project using Max's equipment, which was available while Max was busy writing his thesis and while I was away during that summer. Although Dave ran an independent research program, including positron annihilation, we shared the lab for about ten years. Dave was appointed as an assistant professor in the department in 1962.

At this time, I had another student, Peter Jones, who had done a master's degree with me and was looking for a suitable project for his PhD research. He wanted to use single crystals, but I knew that nobody had been able to observe an NMR signal with such material. Due to the "skin effect" in metal, the signals were very weak. As soon as Dave arrived and started coming to our seminars, he said, "I've got a solution for this problem." He knew it was easy to slice single crystals and glue the different slices together, greatly increasing the total surface area, and that this process would produce material from which we would get a signal. As long as the space between the slices was less than what is required by the "skin effect," it worked. With Dave's help, Peter successfully completed the research for his PhD and went on to obtain a post-doc in Japan followed by another one at Columbia University. He eventually became a physical oceanographer at Dalhousie University.

Frank Curzon, Roy Nodwell, Adam (Hannes) Barnard and Peter Smy formed the plasma physics group within a year or two after I arrived, and they were actively competing among themselves for the chairmanship of the group. Roy Nodwell was appointed the first chair, and they were soon joined by Luis Sobrino and Boye Ahlborn. Luis Sobrino also worked with the theoretical group since he had interests involving general theoretical questions. Maurice Pryce, who came several years later, was also interested in general theoretical physics. In my opinion, he was the most knowledgeable and best-known physicist at UBC.

At this time, around 1960, it was believed that plasma physics had the potential to be useful as a source of energy. However, the ionized gases in plasmas are unstable, and one of my colleagues tellingly observed that although the solution to the formidable problems of plasma stability would eventually be found, the predicted date depended on the age of the observer: it could be five years or twenty-five years—generally the same time as the observer's projected longevity, provided there was sufficient governmental support. A lot of good work has been done, connections have been made with other fields and the problems are much better understood, but plasma physics is not yet a reliable source of energy.

There was also an active nuclear physics group headed by John Warren. Others who joined this group in the next few years were George Griffiths, Erich Vogt, Mike Craddock, Garth Jones, Karl Erdman, Bruce White, David Axen, Ed Auld, Roger Howard, David Measday, Peter Martin, Ken Mann and Doug Beder. Some of these researchers eventually changed focus to work in particle physics. The most important of these appointments was Vogt because he had ambitious ideas about the direction the group should take, and these eventually led to the formation of TRIUMF, Canada's national laboratory for particle and nuclear physics which is based at UBC. Before Erich was appointed, the political struggles between nuclear physics and other groups in the department had at times been acrimonious. However, he had a way of getting people to look at the issues and recognize what the entire department could gain from having a facility like TRIUMF. And after Volkoff took over as chair, he provided the kind of support that made it possible for Erich to carry out his program. They went in the direction of providing intermediate energy, which was more appropriate to a country like Canada and automatically includes connections that bridge the gap between low-energy physics and high-energy physics.

To the surprise of the skeptics, TRIUMF did more than

provide tools and techniques for the study of intermediate-energy physics. It attracted Jesse Brewer, who had just completed his PhD and had quickly become a leader in the field of mu mesons. Jesse led the effort to use the positive muons provided by the TRIUMF accelerator to study condensed matter systems. The resulting technique, muon spin resonance (MSR), turned out to be an extremely important tool in condensed matter systems.

David Balzarini, who came to UBC in the late 1960s, developed powerful optical interferometric techniques that put the university on the map in the field of critical phenomena, an important research area in the 1960s and 70s. The spectroscopy group had people with interests in atomic and molecular spectroscopy, as well as astrophysics. This group included Bill Dalby, Arthur Crooker, John Eldridge and Irving Ozier. Herbert Gush determined the cosmic black-body radiation, and this work was carried farther by Mark Halpern. In my opinion, Herb Gush's measurement was the single most important experiment carried out by one physicist at UBC.

New people coming in to the department each year made forming transient clusters of creative interaction possible. I feel as though I had the right sort of background to promote this kind of collaboration and I wrote papers with other members of the department on a variety of topics. Eventually, the faculty in the physics department numbered more than fifty, and it was important that many of them were very good teachers who were prepared to devote a lot of time to developing new courses such as engineering physics and forestry as well as specialized courses like the physics of music developed by Bill Unruh, a high-profile researcher in quantum physics and cosmology. I sat in on some lectures given by Luis Sobrino in a course on non-linear thermodynamics and the origins of life. Among the group who did so much teaching were Erich Vogt, Mike Crooks, Paul Sykes, Betty Daniels and Roger Howard. Eventually Betty and Roger decided to get married, which provided the department with a good opportunity to celebrate.

I gave two honours courses shortly after I started teaching. One of them was a third-year course in thermodynamics that I gave because I wanted to present material at the high level of science I had seen in the KO lab in Leiden. The other was a fourth-year course in quantum phenomena as well as relativity theory. I started by following the standard introduction given for such a course in North American universities but I found the material weak in the area of quantum mechanics so I switched my emphasis to the two-level (spin-½) system and treated the quantum mechanics thoroughly. I didn't know why the study of this material was traditionally postponed until students were in a graduate program. However, while I was developing this fourth-year course, *The Feynman Lectures on Physics* textbook was first published, where Feynman introduced quantum mechanics in the way I preferred. Within a couple of years, this kind of course appeared in most undergraduate honours programs; mine were well received and always had good enrollments. Graduate students who came from other institutions and did not have enough background in modern physics were also required to take my fourth-year course.

I also did some teaching during the two summers I had spent working in the Los Angeles area, 1961 and 1962. At that time, I was a consultant for an oil company and I gave the employees a course on nuclear magnetic resonance. We also wrote a paper, "Nuclear-Free Precession in Very Low Magnetic Fields," on the use of low-field NMR in the search for good places to find oil in the ground. This involved the detection of NMR signals, which are different when they come from water in the ground as opposed to oil.

Norman Ramsey was one of the early pioneers in NMR. He had been a colleague of Purcell at Harvard at the time I was applying to graduate schools in the US and I met him again when he came to UBC to give a seminar in 1962. He was interested in hiking on Grouse Mountain, and Volkoff also like mountain walks so he suggested we invite one of the graduate students too. I invited Walter Hardy, and the four of us drove to the ski area and hiked from there to the top of Goat Mountain. By then, Volkoff had been appointed head of the physics department and he took the opportunity to talk with Ramsey about problems regarding competition among universities for top graduate students. Ramsey said there was an agreement among physics departments in the US not to offer fellowships or teaching assistantships before April in any year, and Volkoff asked if there were ever violations of this agreement. Ramsey said that Illinois had been caught red-handed about ten years earlier when a student who had applied to both Harvard and Illinois withdrew his application from Harvard before the deadline, saying that he had been offered a fellowship at Illinois. We all had a good laugh when I told them I was that student, and I ended up being supervised by Charlie Slichter, who had been one of Purcell's students.

The physics department at UBC was attracting interesting graduate students when I started there, and I began my research program with some outstanding students. Everyone who joined my group influenced my research in a manner that reflected his or her own creativity and I learned a lot from my students. NMR was one of the least-expensive areas in which to do scientific research, and this made it attractive to students, especially before NMR spectrometers became commercialized. It attracted people who enjoyed building their own complete spectrometer, although each one represented a compromise between experimental skill and scientific taste. At that time NMR was also known as radiofrequency spectroscopy below 100 MHz, and I had built a pulsed phase-incoherent NMR rig to get started quickly. My first few students felt they could improve on the design and they usually did. My first graduate student, Erich Sawatsky, had already enrolled in master's-level courses and was looking at options for his thesis. The topics I suggested further explored the ferromagnetic materials I had worked with at the KO lab, and he went on to do his master's and his doctorate with me.

Walter Hardy was already in the department as an undergraduate when I arrived, and because he had a first-class average, he was able to proceed directly to his PhD. Walter was also an outstanding concert pianist and had won a provincial competition. His wife was also a concert pianist, and they had two children. He enjoyed both music and physics, and I could see he would be an excellent physicist and told him so. That encouraged him to continue in physics. It was a pleasure to have Walter as a student, as he enjoyed the student-teacher interplay and got along well with the electronic and mechanical technicians who helped with the equipment. I had suggested a problem he might work on that I thought was too difficult, but he saw it as a challenge and very quickly overcame the issues.

Max Lipsicas, who contacted me as I was arriving to join the faculty, came with some experience working in industry in Britain and he already knew what kind of research he wanted to do. We had to know how to deal with NMR at high pressure and different temperature levels. He found it useful to break these issues down into a series of instrumentation problems, each of which required a certain amount of time. When we needed equipment, he was able to identify whether such equipment already existed or whether we would have to build it. His habit was to be efficient when he needed to make use of people in the various shops to build those instruments. For example, we would benefit from using coherent radio frequency fields but we had not learned how to manipulate their production and detection. I knew, from interactions at meetings, that such equipment was being developed at other labs, and pretty soon it became commercially available. This was 1960, at least ten years before anyone realized that NMR could have medical applications. Another early graduate student was Harbhajan Singh Sandhu, who studied changes in molecular orientations of hydrogen fluorides.

I was motivated to study molecular hydrogen because the work at Leiden by Bloembergen had shown that the width of the NMR line in the gas varied slowly with temperature at constant volume, over the range 100K to 300K. Such relative temperature independence was inconsistent with the hard-sphere model of molecular hydrogen, which was the accepted theory at the time. I decided to investigate a more fundamental model for nuclear spin relaxation in gases. It was well known that molecular hydrogen had two species, ortho-hydrogen and para-hydrogen, as a result of the quantum-mechanical permutation symmetry property. I decided to check whether the relative temperature independence might reflect the variation of the two species' concentrations with temperature. Max Lipsicas had the same idea, and we were attracted by the problem because it involved very weak inter-molecular interactions and required NMR for its solution.

The equilibrium population of ortho-hydrogen at room temperature is 75 per cent of all the molecules, but at low temperatures it is only about 1 per cent. It is possible to prepare samples of H_2 with any desired proportion of ortho- to para-hydrogen, and by looking at many samples with different proportions, we recognized that the two gases had different NMR properties. Walter Hardy worked at lower densities, where the experimental work is much more challenging. To my surprise, he produced results that contributed greatly to the theoretical model I was then working on with Irwin Oppenheim, who was at MIT. The model we developed made me realize that at low temperatures we were only seeing the effect of collisions involving ortho-hydrogen, which explained the relative temperature independence. This theoretical model was also useful to explain observations on a wide range of molecules, and my team made many measurements that validated the theory.

One day I got a telephone call from a very eminent Polish researcher, Roman Smoluchowski, then at Princeton. He had a question about the diffusion of heavy molecules such as deuterated hydrogen, and Tom Carver, with whom I had done some work at Illinois, had told him I had done the most progressive work in that area. He had spent years developing a model regarding a certain planet and needed to know more about the diffusion constant of heavy hydrogen. I gave him some numbers and realized that by studying something in the small regions of a test tube, you can draw conclusions about the major activity of a planet. This was thrilling. When I set out on this study, I had no idea it would include planets!

I'm sometimes asked what sort of high people get from research and it's easy to say something about ego, but I think there's something more universal that doesn't involve an ego trip. When you come across something important, there is a certain thrill in knowing you're the first one to ever think about things in this way. You may be sitting in a lonely laboratory when you discover something unusual, but when you realize very few people could've made the same discovery because they weren't asking the sort of questions you were asking, that's a very satisfying feeling. I remember when I gave George Volkoff my statement for the encyclopedia of NMR, he came to me after he read it and he said: "You still have got fire in the belly." What he was expressing was that you feel the world poses some problems for you, and if you have fire in the belly you go after them and try to solve them.

When I arrived at UBC, before he took on all the administrative responsibilities for the department, George and his students were still doing creative research. It is possible that he and Oppenheimer might have shared a Nobel Prize for his PhD research if Oppenheimer had not died so young. (Nobel Prizes are not awarded posthumously.) But by the time I met him, George told me he'd lost that fire in his belly.

Maurice Goldhaber, an outstanding physicist, once described his experience with a near-miss when he was working with Enrico Fermi in Rome. He said something like, "You can get fixated with what you're looking for and make the wrong move." He was referring to his experience working on the absorption of neutrons in nuclear reactions. Fission, the absorption of neutrons by a heavy isotope like thorium or uranium, sets up a kind of vibration, and it was a hot subject in those days. Goldhaber found that he got a lot of noise in his detector when he brought the neutron source up from whatever radioactive place it was being kept, but if he put an absorber there, like lead, he could make the noise go away, seemingly diffusing it into random decays. He couldn't find what he was looking for, so he gave up his experiment. Later, someone told him the "noise"—fission—was the result he was looking for; he just didn't recognize it. He was saying all he had to do was interpret the reaction reasonably quickly and he would've gotten a Nobel Prize for it.

I'm sure most people who do research of the type we

do would have had this kind of experience. All you have to do is go down the list of discoveries and some of them will undoubtedly have the aura of coincidence. Serendipity—maybe that's the word that could be used.

CHAPTER 7.

A MERGER:
PHYSICS AND BIOLOGY

I've taken a total of four sabbatical leaves, and each one had a profound influence on my research. The first leave was split between Harvard and Kyoto, in 1964–65. I had a Guggenheim Fellowship during that year, as well as ongoing grants from the Killam Foundation, NRC and NSERC. I decided that instead of starting on new research, I would spend some time summarizing the theory of spin-lattice relaxation. Irwin Oppenheim was at MIT, and I spent one day a week with him. By the end of the academic year we had completed a review article entitled "Intermolecular Forces Determined by Nuclear Magnetic Resonance," which was published in *Advances in Chemical Physics*. I found Irwin to be an impressive and enjoyable collaborator.

When we had parted company in Leiden, the NMR theory had a general formula for spin-lattice relaxation time in an ideal gas. In the time between leaving Leiden and working with Irwin during that sabbatical year, we had continued to develop the theory and published a series of papers with our graduate students. Irwin participated in the experimental work with a group at MIT led by John Waugh, with whom we had a friendly competition. Over about seven years, we were able to provide our PhD students with a series of research programs to develop a foundation for this theoretical advance.

In our review article, we solved the equations for the change in nuclear magnetization accompanying the changes in positions and momenta of the individual colliding molecules. To solve these equations, we replaced the actual changes in the momenta of the individual molecules with those which would be observed if the molecules reaching a second set of positions and momenta had travelled in a straight line with constant acceleration. We called this approach to problems in the kinetic theory of gases "the constant acceleration approximation," and it aroused considerable interest. We felt we had created a quantitative approach to the theory of NMR relaxation in gases and we went on to develop a similar approach for liquids and dense gases and, along with our graduate students, published several papers for different materials.

At Harvard I also consulted with a highly regarded young professor of chemistry, Roy Gordon, who had shown connections between NMR studies of gaseous and liquid methane and other spherical top molecules. I wrote a 100-page review article that appeared in the proceedings of a conference of the International Society of Magnetic Resonance (ISMAR), and this article caught the interest of several NMR and infrared spectroscopists because it accounted theoretically for a wide range of temperature observations over which the spherical top molecules exhibited very little variation of frequency.

I had another reason for wanting to go to Harvard. Researchers there had a lot of expertise with beam experiments, and with Karl Erdman, a nuclear physicist at UBC, I had published a paper entitled "The Transverse Stern-Gerlach Experiment." One of my graduate students, Eric Enga, had demonstrated outstanding ability as an experimentalist, and he was interested in another experiment with this kind of equipment. As a result of my interactions with the Harvard experts, including the Nobel Prize winner Norman Ramsey, I was able to help Enga design a Stern-Gerlach experiment that he could carry out in a reasonable amount of time to complete his PhD research. We published the results in a paper, "Observation of the Transverse Stern-Gerlach Effect in Neutral Potassium."

I thought it might be possible to design a Stern-Gerlach experiment on ions, and Tom Knott, who was completing his PhD at Harvard while I was there, applied for a post-doctoral fellowship to work with me. I accepted him conditionally, the condition being that he explore the feasibility of carrying out the transverse Stern-Gerlach experiment on charged particles. I had never imposed such a condition on a post-doctoral fellow and I promised to remove this condition if he demonstrated that the experiment was too difficult for us to carry out. Tom Knott was an unusual person and he accepted my condition. He did enough work on the Stern-Gerlach experiment for ions to publish a paper where he confirmed that Eric Enga's work on ions, which he completed after his earlier work on neutral potassium, represented a rediscovery of "strong focusing of charged particle orbits in accelerators."

I was thrilled to join those who had made contributions to the understanding of quantum phenomena by making those measurements. For example, Niels Bohr had assumed that we could not produce a state in which the magnetic moment of a charged particle was quantized. Bohr had restricted himself to states having the direction of the spin axis perpendicular to a large magnetic field and had neglected the states having the spin axis parallel to such a field. In the Stern-Gerlach experiments done in my lab, we demonstrated that when you pass a particle through an inhomogeneous field, the spread of the deflections due to the Stern-Gerlach forces was much less than due to the Lorentz forces. This generated some excitement as well as further research because it was not consistent with what Bohr had predicted.

In Kyoto, I gave a review talk on the relationship between the chemical potential (or diamagnetic shift) and the interaction responsible for free-lattice relaxation. I also resumed my relationship with Professor Kubo, who had visited the department in Vancouver on at least two occasions, at a conference in Tokyo. Kubo and I did some work with the well-known professor Kazuhisa Tomita who had worked with Kubo to develop a linear response model for NMR. Tomita had been working independently of Kubo, and it so happened that his work and mine on the quantum theory of relaxation times for certain mixtures of isotopic molecules overlapped.

I also had the opportunity to talk with Professor

Yamamoto in Chemistry about our mutual interests. One day as I was walking down the street, someone tapped me on the back and said: "So you made it! And I see that you have survived the high temperature of a Kyoto summer!" I had met Professor Yamamoto at a meeting in Washington, DC, earlier that year when we had been seated at a table with ten other people. There he had been stiff and formal but invited me to visit him in Kyoto. In Kyoto, he was welcoming and I discovered he was very interested in my work because he was studying phase transitions in molecular methane and I had recently published some papers that he found useful. When I returned to UBC after this sabbatical, I continued with the Stern-Gerlach work and the study of molecules such as ethane and methane. Methane has a tetrahedral structure and is interesting to study, especially in the solid phase. Our study of methane and its deuterated modifications gave an understanding of the quantum nature of the rotational energy states. This kind of investigation requires a meticulous approach, and my graduate student, Peter Beckmann, handled it well.

The work on low-temperature methane attracted Shlomo Alexander, a physicist from the Hebrew University in Jerusalem who was visiting UBC. He wrote to ask if I could find a visiting faculty salary for him and I was able to support him for one year. However, I mentioned to Maurice Pryce that he was interested in staying for another year, since his wife was completing a PhD in economics at UBC, and Maurice said that we should not miss the opportunity to have him stay because Shlomo was an inspiration to the entire theoretical group. Consequently, he was able to assemble a package involving teaching duties and research funds for Shlomo's second year and we profited from the high quality of Shlomo's work because he was such a profound thinker.

I continued to work on critical phenomena, as a material went from the gas to liquid phase or the reverse and from paramagnetic to anti-ferromagnetic for cobalt chloride. I kept working on gases, liquids and solids that were of the same order but gradually increasing complexity and I could have kept myself busy this way for the rest of my life. We made a lot of progress in improving the experimental apparatus, and this made it possible to keep producing more experimental observations of this kind. Other scientists, such as Bernard Shizgal and Brian (B.C.) Sanctuary, both theoretical chemists in the Department of Chemistry at UBC, had a natural interest in the kind of molecules we were studying and they made further observations with their own graduate students.

Around 1970, I was the chairman of the Magnetic Resonance Gordon Conference, held biennially at various New England private schools. After the sessions, there is a banquet and the after-dinner talks emphasize the spirit of the conference, which is to encourage innovation. These presentations do not have to represent research that has appeared in refereed journals, so it's an opportunity to hear about work being done at the frontiers. On this occasion, I was able to persuade Purcell to talk about an experiment that he and Ramsey had done on themselves. Each of them, in turn, had put his head in the coil of an electromagnet while the other one tuned it to the NMR frequency. The one with his head in the coil tried to think about various things to see what sensations he might experience. They did not find any effects, but everyone enjoyed his talk about this "frivolous" experiment.

In addition to my work with the Gordon Conference, I spent five years on committees supported by the Canadian National Research Council (NRC). Almost all Western countries use peer review of some kind to decide how to obtain the most satisfactory results in scientific research. At the end of World War II, there was practically no research going on in Canada and so E.W.R. Steacie, who became a director and then president of NRC right after the war, initiated a large and expensive program of post-doctoral fellowships which supported research for scientists at Canadian universities, as well as for Canadians doing post-doctoral research elsewhere. The travelling grant that supported my work in Leiden was one of those fellowships. Once I started at UBC, I was eligible for equipment and operating grants that enabled me to start my own research program. These grants were available only to people who had a regular university position; in other words, a position that involved both teaching and research.

There were some political issues in administering these grants, since universities in Canada are funded provincially and the NRC program was federal. For a number of years, this federal money was paid directly to the universities but eventually it became incorporated into the transfer payments from the federal government to the provinces. Some non-trivial issues involved geographical and language considerations, since some provinces financed research more generously than others. However, the NRC committees were advised to ignore these issues. During my service with NRC, the average number of members on the mainline physics committee each year was nine and, in general, each year three members came on and three came off. To create a balanced committee, I had been advised a year in advance that I would be expected to chair the committee during my third year. However, I was asked to stay on as chair for an additional year and then I served as chair of the high-energy committee during my fifth year with NRC. I had always been interested in high-energy physics, and I found it rewarding to chair this committee.

In fact, the level of funding needed by various areas of physics research is different, and this was one of the problems that the committee responsible for dispensing funds had to deal with. Different committees reviewed the proposals from the various branches of physics, such as high-energy physics, nuclear physics, geophysics, etc., and in some cases the proposals had to be considered by more than one committee. For example, the proposals involving high-energy physics had to be reviewed by both the accelerator specialists and the high-energy committee. The nuclear physics committee had been reviewing plasma physics proposals starting in the early 1960s, but NRC changed the funding procedures during the time I served on the committee and began to treat these proposals on the basis of individual researchers rather than groups. The result was that support for some groups went down, but they managed to survive.

Projects supported by these NRC grants were evaluated on incremental progress. For continuing projects, the committee had to make judgments such as whether a one-year grant or a three-year grant would be appropriate or whether funding should be continued and for how long. Sometimes it could be more advantageous to earn a one-year grant because when the first year's work was well recognized it could lead to a second year with a higher level of funding. As might be expected, members of the committee often disagreed, though everyone felt free to express their concerns and in the end there was a vote. Universities developed other sources of funding as well, and projects that did not receive NRC funds often survived.

Sometimes, the committee took a risk in granting funds. For example, a proposal from the University of Regina to develop a sensitive detector for gravitational radiation was supported during my last year on the committee. However, eventually support for this project had to be cancelled, much to the disappointment of the physics grant selection committee, when the underlying difficulties simply proved too great for such a project to succeed at a small university.

As I was wrapping up my time on the NRC committees, there was starting to be a lot of exciting activity in connection with the possibility of using NMR to study the biology of membranes. In my work with gases, liquids and solids, the emphasis was on symmetry properties, and I had made a connection with molecular spectroscopy and this kind of symmetry. Biological systems have more subtle kinds of symmetry and are therefore much more challenging to analyze. As I became more interested in such applications, I had concerns about providing useful research projects for my graduate students. I knew that the best way to learn something is to teach it, so I offered a reading course that met once a week for anywhere from one to several hours. Alex MacKay and Robert Clark were master's students and they wanted to work with me *because* I was working in a field that had important biological applications. There were no biophysics faculty members at UBC at that time. We read some recent papers, including controversial articles by Freeman Cope and biochemical material by Mildred Cohn, who was spending a year at UBC with her husband, Henry Primakoff, a well-known theoretical physicist on leave from the University of Pennsylvania. We also did some experimental work. Bob Clark eventually became a biophysicist and Alex MacKay completed a PhD in NMR at Oxford and was then awarded an NSERC fellowship to do post-doctoral work with me beginning in 1975.

In the summer of 1970 I attended a scientific meeting in Paris, and I visited the Abragam lab in Orsay. At the end of that day, I was standing in the station waiting for my train back to Paris when I heard a familiar voice. It was Gil Clark, whom I had known when we were both graduate students, and he had just completed a year as a post-doctoral fellow in Orsay. He was at Cornell working with Don Holcomb, a former student of Slichter, at the same time I was at Illinois working with Slichter. We knew each other well because we were working in the same field, and I thought very highly of him. In fact, we had invited him to apply for an assistant professorship at

UBC the previous year, and I will never forget his visit because it was interrupted by the horrible news that RFK had been assassinated.

As we waited for the train, I told him that I was planning to take my next sabbatical in France and that I had originally thought I might spend it in Abragam's lab. However, whereas I had found it to be lively on previous visits, I was disappointed with the current atmosphere and was thinking of searching for another lab. Gil understood my feelings and said that I should seriously consider spending a year in Orsay because Pierre-Gilles DeGennes was there, and the atmosphere in his lab was very exciting. He told me that they were working on potassium palmitate, which was a model for biological membranes, and that a team of people was working on such molecules.

I had earlier met DeGennes at a conference, where each of us had made a presentation. He jumped into a bus that was conveying conference participants to various locations, sat down next to me and said that he was interested in talking about my results. He wanted to know about a particular ratio and whether I appreciated that it might be an example of critical behaviour in the system whose transition was being studied. In fact, until he made this observation, neither I nor the other experts I had worked with had been aware of any such significance in the results. However, DeGennes was familiar with some new theoretical work, and our conversation prompted me and my group to begin a series of new measurements when I returned to Vancouver.

I took Gil's advice and returned to Orsay the next day

to visit the Laboratoire de Physique des Solides, where I received a warm welcome from its director, Jacques Friedel, and the director of the low-temperature NMR group, Jacques Combrisson, as well as Paul Rigny, a professor of chemical physics at Université de Paris-Sud, and his graduate student Jean Charvolin. Charvolin was eager to have me join the group because of my experience in relaxation time measurements in a wide range of molecular solids and liquids, and it was agreed that I would share an office with him during my sabbatical leave in 1971–72. In the end, I decided to spend two days per week at École Normale Supérieure (ENS) in Paris and three days per week at the Université de Paris-Sud. We lived just south of Paris, near this relatively newer campus, which was very strong in science, and physics in particular. I did share the office with Charvolin, who was applying NMR to the study of liquid crystals. Lyotropic liquid crystals are of special interest in biology. Such crystals are formed when fatty acyl chains are combined with positively charged alkali ions, such as lithium and water. And at the time that I spent my year in France, scientists were beginning to realize that the membranes that surround the cell have structure and define the boundary of the cell but that they are fluid.

This initial research into the structure of membranes was conducted as part of work on the fluid mosaic model of membranes. The basic work on this kind of molecule was done by cell biologists S.J. Singer and G.L. Nicolson who noted that about half of the molecules are amphiphilic, which means they have a hydrophobic part that consists of long acyl chains bonded to a hydrophilic part that can bond with polar molecules such as water. Soap is a simple example of this kind of molecule, and Charvolin was working on the structure of soap.

The NMR research provided information about the symmetry of such molecules and the position of some of the components of the molecular structure. Since such molecules are in constant motion, and the crystal structure has a tetrahedral lattice, NMR reveals how the molecules are moving within such lattices, which in turn tells us about the structure of the membrane under study. Charvolin made the biggest advance in delineating how liquid crystalline properties influenced the nature of the physics, which, ultimately, led to new work on the influence of the isotopic mass of hydrogen, when researchers replaced the protons with heavy protons called deuterons. This isotope of hydrogen is called deuterium. At that time, there was a little competition between researchers in this field, and competition, like war, gets things done. Joachim Seelig, who was based in Basel, Switzerland, started working intensely on the deuterium problem in biological systems and the early developments in going from the liquid crystalline systems led to further insights in biology. The reason deuterium was so important is that it is used to analyze the structure of proteins.

During my year in France, I was asked to be a member of the examining committee for the dissertation of Jean Charvolin. This was an honour, as some of the top scientists in France, such as Jacques Friedel and Vittorio Luzzati, who had done a complete study of structural symmetries for lyotropic liquid crystals, were also on this committee. I also had many opportunities to interact with

DeGennes, who had stimulated the questions that led to Charvolin's research. He was the inspiration I was looking for. He had a very prestigious appointment at the Collège de France that allowed him complete freedom to do whatever he wanted to, and there was a lot of excitement about his group. He was aiming his insights into the study of biological systems and had set up a kind of "esprit de corps" in Orsay, where people were talking to each other a lot. It was his charisma and brilliance that brought people together. Whenever he started working in a field, he attracted experimentalists who wanted to get into that field and he left behind those who had been attracted to the previous field in which he had worked. At the time I met him, he had strongly influenced the fields of magnetism, critical phenomena, phase transitions and liquid crystals and was exploring the biological physics of soft materials. He later won the Nobel Prize for his work on soft tissues.

DeGennes drew almost everyone he came in contact with into his orbit because he was such a charming man and had real insight. He managed to give people the impression that they were capable of understanding the complicated field of biology starting from physics and chemistry. I was no exception, and my own research began to move more in the direction of biological science as described by physics. Even his family was involved: he co-wrote a book about liquid crystals with the mother of his younger children, as well as a book on polymers. His study of polymers involved new mathematical methods and somehow his influence created the spirit of the field. His wife was also a wonderful cook, and while the children were growing up, she developed a restaurant in their house where you could go for lunch and get very good meals. And if you were working in his group, you'd inevitably find yourself invited to his home for dinner.

There's always a lot of excitement when new concepts are being developed. Thinking back on it, clearly DeGennes influenced people to make these leaps of thought but how it all happened is a little hard to define. When you heard him speak it all seemed very natural, but he was making big jumps and sort of felt his way to progress. And people circled him like scavengers to get the benefit of his insights. Some of these more concrete benefits would surface during the discussions that took place after a new experiment. He didn't necessarily make all the leaps himself, but he certainly got rid of the chaff.

At the end of my sabbatical year, Peggy and the children returned to Vancouver in early May. I stayed on in France for six weeks to attend a summer school at Les Houches, organized by Philippe Devaux and other French scientists, including molecular biologists, that brought together people from different disciplines who worked with specialized techniques. I had given up the lodgings in Orsay and moved into a small apartment in Paris, l'Hôtel des Grands Écoles. At one point I told the proprietor, Madame Fortin, that I would disappear for possibly a week and that she should not worry about me. She said, "But Mr. Bloom, you should not pay rent for accommodations that you do not use." I responded, "But I noticed that your hotel is always fully booked and I want to have a place to stay when I get back. And Mr. Alexander will also be visiting Paris and will require a place to sleep." She said, "Don't worry. Just let me know on the day that you return and I will make sure that you have a place to sleep."

When I returned to UBC in 1972, I began charting new territory by focusing on the biological applications of NMR. This followed naturally, because, as a result of my year at Orsay, I had become more interested in bio-physics, which was a focus on biology using physics and chemistry. That year I became one of the founding members of a new biomembrane discussion group that met weekly. Speakers from different disciplines would explain their fields to each other, and this went on for a couple of years. Unfortunately, when I shifted to using NMR in biological settings, I started to have trouble attracting graduate students with a physics background. They were well prepared to do applications in physics but they didn't feel competent to work in biology—even though their physics teachers told them they would be able to. And they didn't feel secure about a possible fallback position, as it was a difficult time to get jobs after obtaining a doc-torate.

I did, however, attract some very talented post-doctoral researchers: Jim Davis was changing from NMR studies of anti-ferromagnetic materials to NMR in membranes; he had a travelling fellowship and he came to work with me because I was doing this kind of work. Marko Valic, a post-doc who had previously done research in Room 100, expressed great interest in the direction I had taken. This persuaded me to apply for funding for a spectrometer with high-powered and phase-coherent radio frequencies which we recognized would be useful in NMR applica-tions to membranes. I received NSERC funding for this instrument and I was also able to obtain a Killam fellowship to support three post-docs. One of them was Marko, another was Tim Higgs, a recent PhD in chemistry, and the third was Chris Nichol, a biologist who was returning to research after a maternity hiatus. Alex MacKay also returned to work with me; he had his own post-doctoral funding from NSERC.

I had other PhD students during this period: Ross Chapman worked on helium-3 (^{3}He), Ian Woods earned an MD after completing his doctorate in ion cyclotron resonance under my supervision and Mike Riggin, who did his undergraduate work at Waterloo, also worked in this area. I did very well at attracting researchers and students from other parts of Canada. Elliott Burnell was a chemist, and he came with a two-year NSERC travelling fellowship to work with me because his PhD thesis had involved NMR in liquid crystals, which was useful background for our membrane studies.

Around 1970, UBC was considering the construction of two new buildings. The physics department had been given the highest priority because we had never had space that was actually designed for physics research. Chemistry also had a high priority. The physics department reviewed the situation and concluded that it was much easier to design a modern teaching building. I was appointed chairman of the building committee, and it was my job to bring forward a departmental proposal. The planning time extended over a few years, during which it became evident that NMR could play an important role in biology and biochemistry. As a result, we felt it was important to promote communication among physics, chemistry and biology, and we wrote a proposal that involved having the three departments share one building.

I first spoke with Gordon Dixon, a biochemist who specialized in molecular biology and had won the recently established Steacie Prize for Natural Sciences. I asked him to find out if there was support in the biology department for a building where scientists in the different disciplines would be able to interact. In fact, I asked him if he would want to move his research into a joint building. He said he'd have to think about it, and a while later he told me that he was interested. My next-door neighbour on Kings Road, Gerald Weeks, was a microbiologist whose research was becoming more and more affected by the Crick-Watson discovery of the double helix genetic structure. He enthusiastically supported having the three departments share one building. At that time there was no direct contact between biology and physics, and after my sabbatical experience with DeGennes in France, I knew how valuable this contact could be.

The chemistry department offered a course called Physical Chemistry, which was and still is the best introductory course to biophysics study at the graduate level at UBC because its mathematical content is accessible to biology majors. The head of chemistry, Charles McDowell, was very pleased to have attracted students in biology and biophysics to chemistry courses, but he strongly opposed the idea of sharing a building, which he apparently considered naive. In the end, a single new building was constructed that was shared by physics and chemistry.

During a period of three or four years, from about 1975, we published some important papers. We were approached by biochemists, biophysicists and biologists, such as Bob Cushley and Jenifer Thewalt from Simon Fraser University and Ian Smith from the National Research Council in Ottawa, who wanted to use deuterium NMR and proton NMR to understand the lipid-protein interaction. For about ten years, this field had been dominated by observations that interpreted that the lipids in contact with the protein were solid, but the conclusion we came to was that for proteins to function, the diffusion of lipids in the structure had to retain fluid properties. Biological cells are enclosed by membranes, and an important function of the membrane is the ability to control the diffusion of material between the outside and the inside of the cell. My team contributed to the understanding that such membranes are composed of lipid bi-layers. There is still some dispute about the structure of lipid bi-layers that contain large amounts of cholesterol. If we had a thin membrane and we introduced a variable amount of cholesterol, for a small concentration of cholesterol the membrane remained thin but with more cholesterol the membrane became thicker.

People working in NMR were confronted with the difficulties of the thin versus thick language used in this context. The most general result of many experiments involving the lipid-protein interaction was that when a membrane protein is longer than the thickness of the lipid membrane to which it is added, both the protein and the membrane will change their dimensions: the protein will become shorter and the membrane will become thicker. However, if the added protein is shorter, then the protein would become longer and the membrane would become thinner.

There were other controversies during this period. For example, Sunney Chan, a professor of chemistry at the California Institute of Technology, was one of the leaders in the use of NMR to study membranes and he observed that the NMR spectrum from lipid membranes contained a narrow NMR line. Ordinarily, a narrow NMR line is associated with very mobile molecules, so he claimed that lipids in membranes contained highly disordered regions. However, I worked out the physics and came to a different conclusion. I suggested that the line shape was what is termed super-Lorentzian, which meant there was no evidence for disordered lipid regions in biological membranes. Our disagreement over this issue persisted for about ten years. We were both invited to a meeting in Taiwan of leaders in modern developments in NMR, where I found that Sunney was chairing the session at which I gave a talk about quadrupolar interaction. I sat down beside him before the session began and asked whether he had read my paper about our disagreement. He smiled and said without hesitation, "I was right, Myer, wasn't I?" What this story illustrates is the psychology of researchers. Chemists tend to use a less rigorous approach, but as a physicist I used more mathematical analysis and was able to get better agreement with the experimental observations.

Another area where this approach proved useful involved the Pake spectrum. George Pake, at Stanford, who hired Bill Little, was one of the first students of Purcell at Harvard and he found an NMR spectrum from the dipole interaction of two spin-½ particles from calcium sulfate and water. This spectrum was called the Pake spectrum, and here is a diagram showing what it looks like.

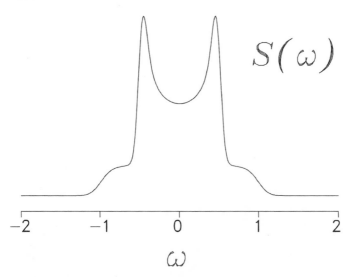

$$S(\omega)$$

$$\omega$$

When you have a protein in water, you have to do motional averaging of the dipolar broadened line, and my team wrote some definitive work showing that the deuterium NMR spectrum has the same form as the Pake doublet spectrum. I was working with Jim Davis and Alex MacKay, and we had made a bet—a bottle of beer—about producing a theory to explain our observations. Someone said that if we could only separate out the dependence on the orientation from that of the other variables, it would be much easier to interpret. I said I thought that was an easy problem and we could solve it, and on the weekend I developed a numerical method. I was the only one who felt it would be straightforward to separate these things, and this was one of the important things we did for applications to membranes. This is now the first step in using deuterium NMR to study the structure of proteins in membranes.

When Purcell was visiting Vancouver in 1978 we discussed this result that we were preparing to publish. Purcell paused for a minute and then said: "Oh that's right, you're de-Pake-ing the Pake doublet," which meant separating out the different contributions by using a numerical trick. These results appeared in two publications: "Direct Determination of the Oriented Sample NMR Spectrum from the Powder Spectrum for Systems with Local Axial Symmetry" and "De-Pake-ing of NMR Spectra." Later, I attended a meeting at Washington University in St. Louis where Pake was being honoured. He gave a talk and he looked at me and said, "Most of you probably don't know what it's like to be de-Paked." It was a comment that conveyed the excitement of our discovery. What I found amusing was that I've actually heard biochemists talking about it on the train or bus saying: "Hey, when we get together, let's go have a discussion about de-Pake-ing." It gave me a kick that these biochemists could get so excited about it without knowing anything about how it was done.

I have to emphasize that Pake's study was made on the spin system arising from two spin-½ protons. The pairs of spinning particles in calcium sulfate are separated by a much larger distance than the separation of the individual protons in a single pair. Therefore, the strength of the dipolar interaction between pairs of protons is much less compared to that between individual protons, and the observed spectrum is that which would arise from an isolated spin-1 nucleus. In deuterium NMR, we are dealing with deuterons, and each deuteron has spin 1. The fact that the spin-1 feature involves only one nucleus makes it possible to eliminate the orientation dependence, which was the problem we set out to solve.

The success of the de-Pake-ing technique brought a series of visiting scientists, including physicists, chemists, biochemists and biophysicists, to UBC to explore the characteristics of NMR spectra under physiological conditions. We did a collaborative study with each set of visitors, who brought samples of materials they were investigating, and they went home and carried out more such studies at their home institutions using commercial spectrometers. The experiments were carried out on two basic types of materials: one involved "model membranes" consisting of pure phospholipid membranes (part A) to which different molecules were added (part B). Deuterium could be added to either A or B using chemical or biological techniques. The other was a natural material such as *E. coli* bacteria. These kinds of studies kept my research team busy from about 1980 to 1990.

CHAPTER 8.

THE ULTIMATE DISCIPLINE IS
INTERDISCIPLINARY

When I returned to France for my next sabbatical in 1978 through 1979, I located myself in the fifth arrondissement, where I visited Philippe Devaux for a good part of the year. He was then a leading French biophysicist. I again had two working locations, one at Orsay with Charvolin and the other in Philippe's lab at the Institut de Biologie Physico-Chimique in Paris. I was given a desk on a fourth-floor balcony overlooking rue Pierre et Marie Curie, which everyone laughingly referred to as my office. This was where I spent most of my time, and it was during that year that I worked out the theory presented in "Squishy Proteins in Fluid Membranes."

In the seven years since my previous sabbatical in Orsay and Paris, a number of researchers had been studying orientational order in model membranes using deuterium NMR. These results did not agree with those that emerged from electron spin resonance experiments. There were disagreements among the researchers about the existence, co-existence or non-existence of immobilized boundary membrane proteins. In the "Squishy Proteins" paper, I proposed a model that could explain the observations and suggested future experiments to test the model.

In France, the most prestigious universities were set up when Napoleon came into power and their purpose was to generate important war weapons. Quite naturally, these same places of innovation also held great potential for promoting the power struggles between countries. Success is largely motivated by power struggles. In fact, if you look at the structure of Paris itself, the main part of the city with its radiating boulevards and arrondissements, it is an artifact of that Napoleonic structural hallmark: *le grand boulevard*. Its original intent was to very quickly move segments of the army in order to control crowds.

During that sabbatical year, we lived on the boulevard de Bonne Nouvelle. All the political demonstrations just marched along the boulevard to make their point. We were also living very close to the headquarters of the Communist Party, and the workers' demonstrations usually took them past that office. There were lots of speeches; it was very high energy. Anyone who lives in Paris sees very quickly that city life is defined in terms of the *quartier*, each individual neighbourhood bounded by the radiating boulevards. Each *quartier* has quite a different character and atmosphere, and after dinner, like all Frenchmen who go for dinner, we liked to walk around and have coffee.

One day, I had invited my friend Philippe to dinner at a Chinese restaurant in the tenth arrondissement because it was of a different style than the Chinese restaurants in the fifth arrondissement where he lived. I noticed that Philippe seemed very ill at ease. Each *quartier* was completely self-contained, and the mannerisms and dress of residents differed noticeably from section to section. He seemed to be taken by surprise; apparently he had not been in that *quartier* for some years.

Towards the end of that sabbatical, Ole Mouritsen wrote to me for advice. He said that he had never studied biology but that he was completing a PhD thesis on theoretical aspects of ordered magnetic systems which he expected to finish before the end of the summer. His supervisor, Knak Jensen, had recommended that he "go to Bloom in Vancouver" because I was working on the structure of lipid molecules, which had high theoretical potential. Ole wanted to know if I would accept him on the basis of a travelling fellowship. He had been told by the people in Denmark who knew his work that his chance of success in receiving such a fellowship was high. I replied that if he won the fellowship, I would accept him. It was my plan to go to Sweden on my way home from France, and I could pass though Denmark on my way to Sweden, which is what I did. I met him and his wife, Kirsten Drotner, in Aarhus and I told him about our research program and how it had been developing. I described to him briefly how promising our research on the Marcelja model for the transition from liquid to solid of fatty acyl chains had become in a short time. I found during my few days in Aarhus that Ole was an intelligent and charming person with broad interests, and it was obvious that he would fit in well if he came to Vancouver.

I felt he should spend the first part of his stay in Vancouver getting to know the interests of the experimentalists and theoreticians, and that he and I should attempt to find an unusual approach to applying physics to important biological problems. There was some interesting research going on in the department. Balzarini was doing experiments on critical behaviour of the gas-liquid phase transition, Burnell was working on liquid crystals, John Berlinsky and Kees de Lange, who was visiting from the Netherlands, were working on high-Tc superconductivity, and Ole spent some time working with these teams. We also had a visitor from Sweden, Hakan Wennerstrom, who was giving a course in which he showed how to include entropy of mixing in treating diffusion when spatially separated different kinds of atoms or molecules are combined.

During this period Jeff Dahn, one of Rudi Haering's graduate students, completed his PhD, and I attended the thesis defence. I suggested to Ole that he might want to look into this, because it involved intercalation compounds where two kinds of forces that played the role of springs and pins in separating or pulling together neighbouring layers had been identified. Ole took the ball and ran with it. We were working with bi-layer membranes that have a similar geometry and we recognized the value of the approach. We developed a useful model, the mattress model, and wrote a paper that was published in the *Biophysical Journal*. The model was successful and generated much additional research.

Ole was only able to stay in Vancouver for two years under his travelling fellowship, and he had originally thought that he might have to become a high school teacher when he returned to Denmark. The success of the mattress model brought him several job offers, and one of these was a fellowship that enabled him to return to Aarhus with good research support. He built up his research group, first at the University of Aarhus and subsequently at the Danish Institute of Technology in Copenhagen. He is currently at the University of Southern Denmark, where he has arguably the strongest membrane research group in Scandinavia, MEMPHYS—Center for Biomembrane Physics.

By the time I took my fourth sabbatical leave in 1985–86, I had four different places in mind. I spent four months in Sydney, Australia; a month at the University of Rome in Italy; two months back with Philippe Devaux's group at the Institut de Biologie Physico-Chimique in Paris; and about two months in Denmark continuing the work with Ole Mouritsen.

In Australia, I worked with Carolyn Mountford's group at the University of Sydney. They had developed an NMR method of detecting cancer but had been unable to publish their work because the medical referees pointed out that there was no theory for the relaxation mechanism proposed. Carolyn had visited my group at UBC in 1984, and in collaboration with Ian Smith of NRC, we had developed a plausible theory. During my time in Sydney, I did some experimental work with them and gave some lectures to explain the theory. After that, Carolyn had no trouble publishing her work. When we were all together at a later date, Australian TV sent a team over to record the drama of our research as an example of the struggle for recognition by female scientists in Australia.

In Rome, I interacted with Bruno Maraviglia's enjoyable team. Bruno had become interested in the results involving biological applications that we were getting at UBC. He was working on medical applications and had visited us in Vancouver. While I was in Rome, I gave some talks on the work we had done with Carolyn Mountford and, later that year, at the Varenna summer school, I gave a short course on NMR in membranes and whole cells, which was based on this work.

I travelled from Rome to Paris by train, and Philippe Devaux met me at the train station in Paris. During the two months in Paris, I worked with Michel Roux in Devaux's group. Shortly afterward he came to continue our research in my lab in Vancouver. We did some important work together, studying the different conformations of phospholipid head groups. Michel was a biochemist, and he was also an accomplished jazz pianist. During his stay in Vancouver, he managed to combine productive sessions in my lab with a full schedule of jazz performances.

In Denmark, I gave a series of seminars and continued some research with Ole at the Danish Institute of Technology in Copenhagen. The work with Ole and his colleague John Ipsen on the relationships between lipid membrane area, hydrophobic thickness and acyl chain order produced a publication that has been used and cited by many other researchers in the field.

The idea of bringing together people who worked in different fields was becoming more and more common.

In 1982, Fraser Mustard founded the Canadian Institute for Advanced Research (CIAR, now known as CIFAR). He had identified areas of complex study, such as astronomy and astrophysics, or evolutionary biology, which might benefit from bringing together outstanding researchers from diverse scientific areas that might have overlapping interests. In the late 1980s I was approached, along with several other scientists, to form a working group on the science of soft surfaces and interfaces (SSSI) because of my publications on biological membranes. One of the really important outcomes of my work with CIAR was that I brought Evan Evans and Michael Wortis together. Evans had a background in engineering physics and had moved into work in biomedical engineering at Duke University before he started at UBC in 1981 under a joint appointment with Pathology and Physics. He came to my talks, and we had discussions about his work on soap bubbles in test tubes, where by changing the pressure he was able to change the bubble shape so that it had wavy characteristics instead of being spherical. Michael Wortis had never thought of working in biology. He was a professor of physics at the University of Illinois until the early 1980s, when he was recruited by Simon Fraser University. I happened to visit the University of Illinois around that time, and Charlie Slichter said that if I could only get him interested, his work on shapes of aggregates of atoms or molecules would be useful in our program.

I went to see Michael and told him we were working on a proposal to CIAR to create an interdisciplinary group to do research on the physics of soft materials, and I suggested he would be a good person to lead the theoretical group. The person I had in mind to lead the experimental group was Evan. I suggested to Michael that he come to UBC to meet with me and Evan and a few additional people to flesh out this proposal, and he agreed to spend a few days doing this. We held an all-day meeting in Vancouver at which the interplay between theory and experiment excited everyone. Our connection with CIAR was very informal—several members of the advisory committee joined the program and vice versa.

The core group consisted of myself, Evan Evans, Michael Wortis, Jaan Noolandi (a polymer physicist at the Xerox Research Centre of Canada), Erich Sackmann (a biophysicist at the Technical University of Munich), Adrian Parsegian (a theoretical molecular biologist from the National Institutes of Health in Maryland) and Theo van de Ven (the director of the Pulp and Paper Research Centre at McGill University). In the next couple of years we were joined by others, such as Terrance Beveridge (a biochemist at the University of Guelph), David Boal (a theoretical biophysicist at SFU), Jacques Prost (the director of the École supérieure de physique et de chimie in Paris), Pieter Cullis (a biochemist at UBC), Ole Mouritsen and Martin Zuckermann (a physicist at McGill who joined SFU after he retired from McGill).

Erich Sackmann was the director of a large biophysics laboratory in Munich, Germany. He had mastered the techniques for characterizing the physical properties of biological materials, and within a short time after NMR was discovered, he recognized its value in this area. I got to know him when he felt that physical techniques for measuring the structure and motion of biological tissues such as membranes were inadequate, and contacted me. He then hired Thomas Bayerl, who had the relevant background, with the condition that he spend a year working with me at UBC. Thomas's wife, Sybille, is also a physicist. She worked in the area of x-ray diffraction and applied her background to study myelin, the coating of nerves. My student, Frank Nezil, had used NMR to study the physical properties of myelin, and Sybille and Frank made important contributions to the paper we wrote together.

Sackmann had students do experiments on changing shapes of such materials, and Evan went to Munich on a sabbatical leave to give a course on biophysics. For a period of about four years, I made annual visits to Munich because the way Sackmann's financing operated made it easy for him to bring visitors to his lab, though it was hard for him to send very many of his students to work with us. Sackmann had a large research budget, and discussions in the coffee room sometimes involved as many as thirty people.

As the program developed over the next ten years, we found that the ease of interaction among various participants, stimulated by our annual three-day meetings, became increasingly productive. By 1996, we had six overlapping sets of participants working on various aspects of the field. We also sponsored a summer school in three different summers for graduate students and post-doctoral fellows, which was judged to have been well attended and highly successful by the CIAR review panel.

Even though I was forced to retire at age sixty-five, the mandatory retirement age at that time, my NSERC research grant continued for a couple of years and I was able to keep the CIAR partial salary until I was about sixty-seven. I had just been diagnosed with Parkinson's disease and I offered to step down as director of the program. However, my colleagues persuaded me to continue, which I did until CIAR discontinued the program in June of 2000 because "underfunding [had been] an obstacle from the beginning." In retrospect, I regret not having fought this decision because we were getting very positive feedback from post-doctoral fellows and graduate students who had participated in our meetings.

I did continue to interact, more and more sporadically as time went on, with several members of the group who continue to do research in this field. Many of them maintained contact for several years and would visit me when they were in Vancouver.

On the weekend of my sixty-fifth birthday, December 5 to 8, 1993, the UBC Department of Physics hosted a symposium at the Château Whistler resort in British Columbia. This was a magnificent event for me—to be surrounded by so many friends and colleagues. It gave me perspective on my career and an opportunity to reflect on what it was all about. Clearly we were celebrating some kind of transition. Actually, in this meeting I realized that my career has involved transitions throughout. To some extent, I was looking for transitions. For example, I always said that my main religion during my career was "every seven years thou shalt take a sabbatical leave." I did this faithfully. In retrospect, all of these sabbatical leaves represented an attempt to randomize the input, and to see if I should take a new direction. Often there would be a delay of a year or two before the effects of these sabbaticals became apparent. However, each leave had a profound effect on my career—I see them now as little accidents, or lucky hazards, that led me in important new directions.

AFTERWORD

Bernice Kastner

I am Myer's sister and I moved to Vancouver in 2005, about two years after Peggy died. I had been widowed myself some ten years earlier, and it seemed to me that this move would be good for both Myer and me. My husband and I had spent a few years in Vancouver in the early 1980s, and I had worked at Simon Fraser University, where I still had some professional connections.

Myer has been working on this autobiography for many years. He started writing it shortly before our family convened to celebrate our mother's ninetieth birthday in December of 1995, but he was still actively involved in his research and had little time to work on the document. In retrospect, that was also the time when the early effects of Parkinson's disease were beginning to appear, though it was several months later that he received the diagnosis. I should mention, in the context of our mother's birthday, that she had written a memoir, *A Letter to My Grand-children*. Our children were very interested in it, and as a result, both Myer and I have tried to follow her example in writing our own memoirs.

The effects of Parkinson's disease on Myer were very much in evidence by the time I got to Vancouver in 2005, and they have continued inexorably since then. In particular, Myer gradually lost the ability to write legibly by hand and, as well, the motor control to manage a computer. When I arrived, he had a wonderful student, Kasia Sowka, working with him on a part-time basis. Kasia was an undergraduate majoring in physics and she understood what he had done in his research life, which also encouraged him to continue the work. After that academic year, however, she left Vancouver for Toronto, where she continued her studies to become a certified teacher of mathematics. She found another student, Briana Lyon, to take over the work of recording Myer's story. Although Briana did not have as much physics background, she was a speed typist and was able to record Myer's story as he told it, with a high level of accuracy. Eventually, however, she graduated and also left the area.

In 2008, Myer had a hospitalization that involved a cardiac arrest; he did recover but he had to move to a residence that could provide the level of nursing care he needed after this setback. His good friends Walter Hardy and Christina Kaiser helped to keep the ball rolling. In particular, they tracked down documents for reference at Myer's request and took dictation, often recording and transcribing Myer's recollections. Eventually, another of his good friends, Don Brown, made a computer equipped with voice-recognition software available to him. With help from Christina and a crucial contribution from Fiona Burnell to train the software to respond to Myer's voice, it was possible for Myer to proceed by dictating to the machine. However, another effect of Parkinson's disease eventually made this method impossible: the voice gets very much softer, enunciation less precise, and the software could not function properly. He maintained his interest in continuing to work on the memoir, and as a frequent visitor, it was obvious to me that the best way to proceed with this document was for him to talk while I typed. This is how I became the "amanuensis" for the writing.

The first thing I had to learn when we began to work this way was to refrain from "helping" when Myer had trouble finding the right words for what he was trying to express. It was quite apparent to me that he has a much more literary writing style than I do, and that he needed to tell his own story in his own way, even when he could not immediately think of the words he needed. In the end, he always found a way to express himself.

I was not at all familiar with the details of his life between 1949, when he left Montreal, and 1982, when my husband and I had arrived in Vancouver. As Myer has mentioned, we were in Syracuse while my husband attended graduate school at just the time when Myer and Peggy had decided to get married, but we had lived in Maryland for most of the time while Myer was in Vancouver, far enough apart to make it hard to see each other very much. Of course, this made the recording of his story quite interesting to me.

Although Myer kept a "Parkinson's diary" for a while after he received the diagnosis, he decided that he wanted to end this memoir at the time of his retirement at age sixty-five. During the course of our work together, I became aware that there are some additional stories to tell, but perhaps Myer is not the one to tell them. He has written about how he altered the focus of his research to develop an interdisciplinary team, but it seems to me that there is likely another interesting story about how he managed the lab to produce the kind of camaraderie that was evident to anyone who visited there.

I was able to attend a seminar series given in Myer's honour in 2007, and the reports presented on this occasion certainly showed me how inspiring the participants had found it to work with him. My guess is that perhaps it was because of what he expressed near the end of Chapter 5, in explaining why he chose to go to UBC instead of working with the leaders of the field in France at that time: "In retrospect, I realize I knew it would be a good idea to escape from all these clever people and give myself room for my own ideas." Maybe what he succeeded in doing was to provide his graduate students and others who came to work at his lab with the space to develop their own ideas.

There is also a story to be told about Myer's grace and fortitude in dealing with the twenty-plus years of Parkinson's disease: the inexorable erosion of his mobility, the steadily increasing dependence on others for the simple tasks of daily life, the side effects of the medication without which he would have no mobility at all, to mention just a few of the difficulties. Never one to make demands or issue complaints, the closest Myer gets to a lament is about his inability to get himself to a restaurant of his choice for a gourmet meal.

ACKNOWLEDGEMENTS

I am grateful to Charlie Slichter, my Ph.D. adviser at the University of Illinois, who managed to combine guidance and inspiration so successfully that it led me into a career in nuclear magnetic resonance. I hope that the story itself shows the many other people to whom I am indebted for inspiration and guidance over the course of my research.

For the writing of this book, I first want to thank my sister, Bernice Kastner, who helped me complete the narrative when it became too difficult for me to physically manage the writing. There were many times when I would have given up without that support. It was wonderful to see how the book chapters filled out steadily with her help. I was transformed by our collaboration, allowing myself to become ambitious again.

Many other people also made invaluable contributions that helped me continue to make progress. I will try to list some of them, though it raises the risk that I will omit some important contributors. I do worry about how

Parkinson's disease has played havoc with my memory, but I must try to recognize as many as I can:

Christina Kaiser and Walter Hardy helped in so many ways that it's hard to keep track, especially after I had to move to assisted living, including recording and transcribing my dictation, providing general computer assistance, sourcing information when needed, and paying frequent visits to take me out and give me a change of scenery;

My niece, Judith Skillman, Bernice's daughter, who assembled the scattered early pieces to form the first draft of the book, and who provided continuing editorial assistance as the work grew;

My former neighbour, Don Brown, Professor Emeritus of the Philosophy Department of UBC, who generously provided me with a computer equipped with voice-recognition (Dragon) software, and Fiona Burnell, who helped make it possible for me to use it;

Walter Hardy, Roger Howard, and Alex MacKay, who gave me feedback on drafts of some sections when I needed this;

Thomas Bayerl, who provided invaluable support from a great distance that helped keep me moving;

Pieter Cullis and Jenifer Thewalt, who took care of the editorial arrangements to get the book printed, and the people who contributed to making this happen, listed below:

Michèle Auger, Thomas M. Bayerl, John Berlinsky, Jess H. Brewer, Elana E. Brief, Pieter R. Cullis, James H. Davis, Evan Evans, Nancy J. Flight, Hans Glättli, Walter N.

Hardy, John H. Ipsen, Kenneth R. Jeffrey, Christina V. Kaiser, Catherine Kallin, C. Neil Kitson, Andrzej Kotlicki, Michel Lafleur, Jamie Lloyd-Smith, Alex L. MacKay, Carl A. Michal, Michael R. Morrow, Carolyn E. Mountford, Ole G. Mouritsen, Irving Ozier, James M. Polson, R. Scott Prosser, Michel Roux, Amy C. Rowat, Ian C.P. Smith, Edward Sternin, Henry J. Stronks and Bruker Ltd., Jenifer L. Thewalt, Brian and Annie Turrell, Lorne A. Whitehead, D. Llewelyn Williams, Michael Wortis, Martin J. Zuckermann and Mariela W. Johansen.

SELECTED PUBLICATION LIST

Bloom, M., and E.L. Hahn and B. Herzog. "Free Magnetic Induction in Nuclear Quadrupole Resonance." *Physics Review* 97 (1955): 1699–1709.

Bloom, M., and L.B. Robinson and G.M. Volkoff. "Calculation of Frequencies and Relative Intensities of Nuclear Spin Resonance Lines in Crystals." *Canadian Journal of Physics* 36 (1958): 1286–94.

Bloom, M., and K. Erdman. "The Transverse Stern-Gerlach Experiment." *Canadian Journal of Physics* 40 (1962): 179–93.

Thompson, D.D., and R.J.S. Brown and M. Bloom. "Nuclear-Free Precession in Very Low Magnetic Fields." *Journal of Chemical Physics* 40 (1964): 3076–79.

Bloom, M. "Intermolecular Forces Determined by Nuclear Magnetic Resonance." In *Advances in Chemical*

Physics: Intermolecular Forces, vol. 12, edited by J. Hirschfelder, 549–99. New York: InterScience Publishers, 1967. doi: 10.1002/9780470143582.ch10.

Bloom, M., and E. Enga and H. Lew. "Observation of the Transverse Stern-Gerlach Effect in Neutral Potassium." *Canadian Journal of Physics* 45 (1967): 1481–95.

Bloom, M. "Squishy Proteins in Fluid Membranes." *Canadian Journal of Physics* 57 (1979): 2227–30.

Bloom, M., and J.H. Davis and A.L. MacKay. "Direct Determination of the Oriented Sample NMR Spectrum from the Powder Spectrum for Systems with Local Axial Symmetry." *Chemical Physics Letters* 80 (1981): 198–202.

Sternin, E., and M. Bloom and A.L. MacKay. "De-Pakeing of NMR Spectra." *Journal of Magnetic Resonance* 55 (1983): 274–82.

Mouritsen, O.G., and M. Bloom. "Mattress Model of Lipid-Protein Interactions in Membranes." *Biophysical Journal* 46 (1984): 141–53.

Bloom, M. "Personal Views of NMR History." *eMagRes*, 2007. doi:10.1002/9780470034590.emrhp0024.